A New Dawn

Finding Joy Amid Loneliness

Paris Bailey

peaceful panda publishing

Mom,
Thank you for all your help with the creation of this book. I love, value, and treasure you.

Roberta,
Forever my friend. You helped me through one of the darkest periods of my life. Thank you for your friendship and support. I will always pick up when you call. One day we will yell
'BINGO' together!

Contents

Introduction   VI

1. Alone vs. Loneliness   1

2. The Blues Ain't Nothing but a Mood Swing   21

3. The Cloudy Days   41

4. Laughing in the Face of Loneliness   45

5. Breaking Up With Isolation   67

6. Chasing Away the Blues   72

7. Life Is an Adventure   124

8. Beating the Blues With a Bigger Perspective   130

9. The Sun Will Come Out Tomorrow   132

10. Embracing the Shadows   135

11. Conclusion   137

Author's Note to the Reader   138

References   139

About Author   151

Introduction

"All great and precious things are lonely."-John Steinbeck

Loneliness can knock on anyone's door or quietly and persistently slip in uninvited—through the tiny cracks of our carefully built walls. Perhaps, cunningly squeezing itself in like a slithering snake, or past the open windows of our unsuspecting hearts, walking in nonchalantly like a lazy pet cat. There'll also be times when it comes at us with a bang—a sharp pang throbbing in your gut or a tight, almost physical pain in your chest, born out of a deep, hurtful past, like a bubbling volcano crater ready to erupt. It can stem from a deep longing for genuine companionship—for that subtle spreading warmth that genuine connections bring—or from missing someone precious: a departed loved one, a lover who slipped away, or maybe a gem of a friend we got cut off from for some reason. Or maybe from memories of rejection and isolation—mental images of endless searching and finding none.

Loneliness can be the only thing left in a vacuum whenever we feel isolated or when we grope through the spaces where someone should have been or would have been but isn't. It is easy to understand at times—such as when we are dealing with loss or isolation—but harder to make sense of occasionally—such as when we catch ourselves feeling lonely in the midst of wonderful people or in moments where we are supposed to be having fun, surrounded by family or friends. Sometimes, loneliness could also spring from a sense of disconnection from our old selves when, all of a sudden, we wake up to the realization that we are no longer who we once were, and we miss that. It has various faces, but it yearns for the same thing: bridges. Relatedness, connection, affiliation, intimacy—no matter how hard we try to convince ourselves otherwise, the depths of our hearts will always come after these things.

It's easy to think that the antidote for loneliness is surrounding ourselves with happy people. Then again, experience tells us it's not always that. More often than not, loneliness has nothing to do with who we are with at the moment—or whether or not we are with anybody, for that matter—but whether or not we have saturated the depth and quality of personal connection we are all hardwired to always seek.

Quite frequently, we hate to admit that we are lonely. Everywhere we go, the world seems to either expect us to build connections and manage relationships like pros, or take on feelings of isolation like it hardly bothers us. So, we put on those smiling faces, buff up our social media accounts with photos suggesting we're well and good, and try to convince ourselves that we are indeed okay. And perhaps we are, on a practical level—breathing, functioning, and moving on. But loneliness likes to seep deep and lie low, grabbing hold of sadness whenever it can and, sometimes, bringing with its self-disgust and guilt too. It likes to hide in the curtains and come out at unlikely times, catching us off guard. Just when we think we've buried it deep, it pokes its head into our business like a neglected young child, eyes pleading, saying, "Notice me," just when we're so close to convincing ourselves it's gone for good.

We all want to be happy. Yet in the face of loneliness, joy can be as elusive as a unicorn in the mist, and the fact that we often run after it without so much as a map in hand makes it even harder to keep up with it. We try to follow it and grab hold of even a glimpse of it, but at times, we keep coming back to where we started without really knowing why. More often than not, trying to figure out why can be even more painful than loneliness itself. So, we often come to the conclusion that perhaps loneliness keeps joy away—that maybe, just maybe, loneliness cannot bear to have joy in the same room and to be truly happy, we've got to get rid of it all at once. And we set out to do exactly that—push loneliness back farther and farther away from consciousness as we distract ourselves with anything that resembles joy—maybe a fun night partying, a nice dinner with family and friends, maybe going on a date or two—but then wonder when, despite all our efforts, we still don't seem happy enough. If anything, our inner space is even emptier without loneliness there.

What we often fail to realize is that it is possible to find joy in the midst of loneliness—yes, joy and loneliness can exist in the same space. If we just let ourselves, these two don't have to cancel each other out. You see, loneliness, at its very core, is an adaptive emotion. It is not an enemy to be subdued. If we let it, it has a lot to tell us about ourselves—what matters to us, what we miss, what we need, who we are, and who we could become. It can tell us about the quality of our present relationships and remind us to seek out solutions or actively and persistently grab every bit of opportunity there is to heal. Loneliness isn't there to punish us or make us miserable; it's there to give us that little nudge to do something about our situation.

As counterintuitive as it may seem, it is possible to transform your experience of loneliness into an opportunity for growth, healing, and self-discovery. You see, the more you gain the courage to feel the hurt that loneliness brings and allow yourself to do so, the more its pain lessens its grip on you, and the more your inner space becomes safe enough for joy to creep back in. There is enough room for joy, even when there is sadness or loneliness there. It's a bittersweet truth we all deserve to know. And all this is far from wishful thinking either. For instance, according to Naomi

Rothman and her colleagues (2021), ambivalence, or the "simultaneous experience of positive and negative emotions about something," is a powerful tool for growth and healing. That is, feeling both pleasant and unpleasant emotions at once is not only possible—it is beneficial. If we would only cling to hope more often than we grab hold of fear, we'd be able to befriend loneliness—perhaps even discover and get to tap that quiet, subtle wisdom it brings with it.

Whether you are just starting your journey or have been struggling for a long time, your pursuit to find joy and fulfillment in yourself, your relationships, and your life again is not a futile one, and this book seeks to help you find the right footing to do just that. Through practical advice, and a wealth of resources, you will discover new ways to connect with others, find purpose and meaning in your life, and rediscover the joy of living. A new dawn of joy, peace, and fulfillment awaits those who sincerely seek it. So, let yourself breathe in that gentle surge of strong hope as you open your eyes to watch the first light of day crack open.

Chapter 1

Alone vs. Loneliness

"I inhale loneliness like it is the sweet smell of virgin earth conquered by fiery raindrops. Within me, I'm a thousand others."-Farazz Kazi

Is that even possible? To be able to see loneliness this way? To soak in its depth and dance with the sadness it is creating so that even painful memories become bittersweet? To resist the urge to turn and run—away from the hurt, away from the parts of us we have come to detest? To risk coming face-to-face with pain? Can we throw ourselves in complete abandon, laying all our guards down? Can we muster that much courage to rid ourselves of the chains and fences that, though originally meant to protect us, have come to hold us as prisoners instead? While all that may have sounded foreign or even strange, those who have known what it's like to befriend the depths of solitude could attest that there is strange comfort there.

When we pause the desire to constantly be with other people, we clear up space for being with ourselves. You see every opportunity to step back and let ourselves soak in the comfort of silence grants us a precious gift—the ability to let ourselves wallow in the depths of the moment's experience, to get to know our vulnerable parts, and fall in love with them; to reconcile with ourselves, and to discover the wealth of strength and potential we all have inside of us. In the end, it is only when we get to step away from the noise of the world that we can tune in to the voices inside of us and realize they aren't our enemies—to console the parts of us that are hurting—and open up tiny cracks in the walls of our dark and tiny attic rooms, to let the sun in—for healing... for hope.

While there is a huge difference between being alone and being lonely, these are two things our minds tend to associate almost automatically. After all, we have been taught to find joy in the presence of others. In fact, society may even go so far as to make us believe that unless we have strong connections with a lot of people around us, there is something seriously wrong with us. But what if we don't have to be the whole world's friends? What if we're actually capable of standing alone? What if it's okay to be an island, at least for a little while, so we can regain the strength to build bridges again? What if, deep down, what truly bothers us is not loneliness but the belief that, in the first place, feeling this way is undesirable or not allowed? And then, what if we just stop seeing aloneness and loneliness on the same continuum?

Aloneness doesn't have to be isolating. It doesn't have to hurt or cut deep. Just as being in the crowd does not guarantee connection, being on your own is not a prerequisite to loneliness. What makes us lonely or not lonely then? Lamia (2011) says it is not the amount of time we spend alone. You see, loneliness is a complex emotion. It does not have a single source, and two lonely people may need entirely different approaches to deal with it. Nevertheless, it has one major root: what the American Psychological Association considers a "perception of aloneness" (Novotny, 2019). This perception has nothing to do with the actual scenario. What we feel inside us can have nothing to do with what is actually happening to us. This is why Holocaust survivor Victor Frankl (2006), also a psychologist, was able to observe that despite extreme physical circumstances, there are still people who survive. "They have the ability to 'escape through their spiritual selves,'" Frankl concluded. And what does he mean by that? Certainly not pretending life's difficult situations don't exist! Rather, that despite all the chaos in the outside world, it is as another Holocaust survivor, Eva Engel, would put it: "No one can take from us what we put into our own mind" (Denning, 2020).

When we cultivate an inner space of harmony and peace, it grounds us in a deeper personal reality of security that is as real as the chaos outside of us. Similarly, when the space inside us is marked by a ranging crossfire, the good things around us are easily obscured. While this does make sense, given that our brains are responsible for telling our bodies how to respond, it can be a hard thing to grasp at first. Because we constantly, maybe unconsciously, associate our inner experiences with our outer situation. We don't always get the fact that, at times, our perception of the world is not as flawless as we'd like. The more we open our eyes to this truth, however, the more we get to separate ourselves from intrusive, negative thoughts. This allows us to differentiate who we are with our emotional experiences. Why allow yourself to become slave to assumptions that, in the first place, most likely stemmed from the brain's information processing autopilot? You have the capacity for thoughtful consideration and logical thinking. Why not take advantage of that? We can be in more control of our inner world than we think, and this space isn't imaginary—it is a huge part of our human experience, and the more we learn to nurture and tend a garden there, the more we find the strength to face the challenges outside of us.

All this said, should we always seek solitude, then? "Not necessarily," as several psychologists would say. "Living with the world requires solitude and company," Peter Jandrick noted. The key is finding the sweet spot, and it's different from person to person. Then again, finding the key is just half the equation, because as soon as you have it, you're going to have to look for the door too.

How to Turn Aloneness Into Something Positive

The circumstances of why we ended up alone and whether or not we personally prefer it also plays a huge part. Rubin and Barstead (2018), for instance, pointed out that alone time can only be truly beneficial when certain conditions are met. First, it has to be one of many options the person has, not a forced choice; and second, the ability to manage emotions and soothe oneself in times of distress should be present. Based on these principles, here are a few tips you may want to try out:

Get comfortable with silence.
While silence is usually associated with peace and tranquility, who hasn't heard the phrase "silence is deafening"? If you're one of those who feel this way about quiet time, try to explore what silence reminds you of—is it, perhaps, something unpleasant? You see, the memories we associate with events influence our thoughts about them, and subsequently, thoughts affect how we are going to feel. Being aware of what quiet times remind you of not only helps you make sense of the whys behind your discomfort—it also helps you to differentiate two situations—the one in your memory and the current event so that you can come to terms with it and see the new situation in a fresher light.

Upgrade your emotion-regulation skills ahead of time.
Don't wait until you're at the peak of emotion before trying to learn the skills necessary to manage it. The best time to learn these is when you are most relaxed, less reactive, and in a literally and figuratively safe place. The common mistake that people make when trying to manage their negative emotions is to only deal with them when they're at an all-time high and forget about skill-building during all those precious, lull

moments in between. This doesn't work because our thinking and feeling processes are operated by different areas of the brain in such a way that, when the brain parts responsible for eliciting emotions are in full work mode, those responsible for reasonable thinking are less active. That said, attempting to figure anything out during the peak of an emotional outburst is like trying to pour water into a jar with the lid closed. So, set yourself up for success by taking advantage of the times you are most likely to absorb and retain what you set out to learn.

Before proceeding to the next tip, here are a few extra things to keep in mind:
First, emotions are physical—yes, when we feel, the state of our whole body is altered. Emotions aren't all in our heads. So, every time you're feeling a lot, pay attention to your physiological responses; they will give you more clues about what you are feeling than any of your automatic thoughts could. Second, ignoring or suppressing emotions in an attempt to manage them is a very poor and potentially psychologically harmful strategy. Every emotion demands attention; ignoring them doesn't make them disappear. It's like sweeping dust under the rug—in no time, it won't be just dust—it'd be an ugly mound of dust and every bit of garbage you wouldn't want in there. This remains a popular approach because it is usually easier and, on the surface, may appear to make logical sense. Also, more often than not, it usually works for a certain period of time. Nevertheless, the effect is rarely

long-lasting, if at all. So, aim for the harder, yet surer route, and never underestimate tiny wins. Remember, these can make a huge difference once they add up.

Deliberately set time to be alone.

The circumstances that led us to solitude largely influence the extent of loneliness we'll feel (Rubin & Barstead 2018). Loneliness, it turns out, doesn't stem from the alone time we deliberately picked for ourselves. As Rubin would put it, "Alone time can only be truly beneficial when the person isn't forced into the situation and when the person is confident with their ability to soothe themselves during emotional turmoil." Rubin pointed out two kinds of solitary individuals, based on their motivating factors: "those who are motivated by fear, the prospects of social appraisal, and heightened sensitivity to the possibility of rejection; and those who have a distinct preference for solitude."

The former tends to end up lonelier, while the latter is more likely to maximize the time for self-development. That said, allow yourself to plan for the alone time ahead. Anticipate alone time even when you expect to be with other people—and don't forget to have your backup solo activity ready. Think of alone time as a treat to yourself instead of a reflection of what others might think of you. If you're not used to solo activities, it's not too late to try some out and see what you might enjoy. Get creative, and don't be afraid to make mistakes—remember, when you're having a date with yourself, you can be as free as a bird. Who knows, this might just be what you need to feel happier, more confident, and more secure.

◆○◆

Overcoming the Pain of Isolation

People generally dislike anything painful, be it emotionally or physically. Whether it comes in the form of a sharp pang or dull throbbing, and whether it presents itself physically or emotionally, our natural human response to pain is to recoil. As Thorndike noted, humans repeat behaviors that are associated with positive experiences and avoid behaviors that are associated with pain (Austad, 2009). Nevertheless, pain isn't an all-time menace. According to MedlinePlus (n.d.), for instance, it serves as "a signal in your nervous system that something may be wrong." That is, it informs the brain that certain needs aren't met. Needs are basic requirements for well-being; they are important, necessary, and prerequisites to surviving the world—definitely not stuff we'd like to take lightly or neglect.

William Glasser (2014) went as far as to say that all of life's pain comes from unmet needs and that all of life's pleasure comes from fulfilled ones. He named five basic human needs—survival, belonging, power, freedom, and fun—and argued that they are interrelated, not hierarchical. In other words, our needs overlap and even conflict with each other at times. Thus, one unfulfilled need is bound to have some effect on your total experience, even when all the others are adequately satisfied. That said, it isn't really hard to tell why isolation hurts a lot: it steps directly into our need for love and belonging, which, in an evolutionary sense, is deeply connected with survival, but not only that. Because needs are interconnected, it can steal our joy in other areas as well.

The very purpose of pain is to make us uncomfortable enough to at least attempt to do something about the situation—to actively fill in what we lack, thereby increasing our chance to cope with life's challenges and, thus, enhancing our overall well-being. Pain is, therefore, a message, not a punishment. So, let the pain remind you that the hurt you have been trying to ignore, shuffle, or get rid of is proof that part of you still fights—no matter how unmotivated another part of you feels. Take it from G.I. Jane who reminds us:

"Pain is your friend, your ally—it will tell you when you are seriously injured, keep you awake and angry, and remind you to finish the job and get the hell home. But you know the best thing about pain? It lets you know you're not dead yet!"

No matter how unpleasant it feels, don't forget that pain's been trying to tell you to do something, even if it's as simple as swinging your feet out of bed just this once, moving a muscle to turn on the shower, or rubbing the first lather of shampoo in your hair after weeks of trying to put it off. So, whenever you feel isolated and it hurts, don't beat yourself up. Listen to the pain—what does it tell you? Feel toward it. Thank it, befriend it, and tell it that you know what it's trying to do and that, no, you're not going to force it out of your headspace this time. Now that's going to be somewhat uncomfortable for a while, but hey, wouldn't you rather hurt to heal than just hurt with no end in sight?

It may take some time, but once you've gotten used to welcoming pain in your headspace as an ally, you can use the information it brought you to do something about your situation. More often than not, pain brings with it other emotions, most of them far from pleasant—anger, anxiety, loneliness, guilt, and probably a lot more you couldn't name. Some people would like to start by sorting these out first, approaching them one by one—or all at once—and coming to terms with them. Others, however, prefer dealing with the practical situation first—decluttering, problem-solving, making small but necessary changes, or exploring and recalibrating their thoughts—because diving right into your emotional layer can be quite overwhelming. It's fine either way. So, be honest with yourself, listen to your heartbeat, mind your intuition, and let your own worries out and acknowledge them. Try to pick a good time and a safe place; turn off your self-doubt and tune into your psyche with curiosity in your heart, not judgment.

Don't take other people's advice too seriously either—at least not until you've checked it against your own goals, values, and desires. You see, despite what a lot of books might say about it, there is really no one way to heal. More often than not, we look for answers outside of ourselves when our true power over the situation lies in our home court—that often-forgotten space inside our mind, a source of insight, creativity, and strength. These are yours for the taking: just let yourself.

———◆○◆———

Embracing the Beauty of Alone Time

Contrary to what our brains want us to think, solitude isn't always dangerous. If anything, it can even be liberating. The world can be so noisy—sometimes enough to choke peace out of our systems. Ironically, we still prefer this over silence. Silence, for most of us, can be quite menacing, awkward, or isolating. We are so used to seeking out that constant buzzing we have grown quite accustomed to—every bit of its familiar lure telling us that all is well, even when it isn't. We all have the capacity to build and harness our inner strength, and with that comes the ability to muster the courage. The kind that is enough to keep us from bolting out the door whenever waves of loneliness cascade into waves of pain—the kind that lets us hold our ground as the weight of solitude ebbs and crashes in its fullness against the walls of our hearts, until every bit of aching melts into warmth and space, the way spring breaks open. But if you've been wrestling with loneliness long enough, you know that wouldn't be easy. You may need to take on a whole new mindset, for one, and this in itself is no easy feat. Nevertheless, difficult is not synonymous with impossible. That is, there will always be a few things you can do on your end, and we can never underestimate the power of what we could do. Once you have changed your mind about being alone, it is easier to make the most of these moments. Here are some things you could do:

Read

A lot of people who enjoy solitude also enjoy reading. If you haven't already, you should go check it out. Forget about not being into books. Forget about not being a good communicator. Forget that you vowed to hate all forms of reading material when your language teacher flunked you way back in third grade. Just pick a book and get started, and be sure to choose one that draws your interest like a magnet. Forget about genre, level, and thickness—all these don't matter as much as whether or not you're enjoying it. For starters, pick the least intimidating ones—those with a simple writing style, a good layout, good paper quality, and interesting content—pamper yourself with the best book you can find, and just let yourself take it in.

Write

"To survive, you must tell stories," says Umberto Eco. And indeed, writing is an amazing way to grow and a powerful way to heal. Anyone who knows how to talk can also write. All you have to do is stop worrying about how it will look, take notice of the reality around or inside you, and let yourself go—and then the words will just pour in. So, whenever you find yourself alone, grab the opportunity to record just that moment—all the joy and sadness of it—or retell a story of your fondest memory.

Write about anything and everything. Write about not knowing where to start or not knowing what to write. Write about your emotions or the people you see from across the street. Describe how your cat looks when you open a can of tuna or how your dog barks like crazy over some random squirrel on the lawn. Write about the ex you miss or the person you are going to marry. Write about your divorce or your mental health concerns. Jot down your dreams or your fears, or describe your favorite song. Let your mind drift, and write about where it takes you. Write freely, unapologetically, and marvel at the world you recreate.

Make Art

Art has healing potential all its own, but people don't get access to it because of this one thing: when we attempt to make art, we often do it with other people in mind—will they like it? While nothing is wrong with the latter, it is the former that opens up the door to personal healing. You see, we are all capable of making art, but the world's standards often discourage us from even trying, making that potential inaccessible to many. We worry about whether or not we are good, and quite frequently, the gauge we use comes from how they commented on our first pieces of work or what we see other people make. Except for a number of us who've gotten past this pretty normal concern, a good chunk of humanity doesn't bother to try making art because "I'm not creative" or "I don't have that talent." But being an artist is not a talent—it is an attitude, and it is this attitude that builds skill.

You see, art is simply allowing yourself to create something—anything—by manipulating objects in the environment. It doesn't have to portray anything realistic, and it doesn't have to be something new. Some artists like to plan ahead—they envision a picture in their heads or pick a nice place to copy, for example, before proceeding with sketching, sculpting, or installation. Others don't plan at all. They just keep adding and omitting things on their canvas or platform until it stops being random and finally speaks to them. What do we mean by art speaking to us? It is when you view something and it reminds you of another or sends a certain feeling through you, like deep peace, controlled discomfort, or a bittersweet heart-string tug. Art can be as simple as a dot or as intricate as a life-like statue of a Luna moth.

The magic of art, just like writing, is that it offers you boundless freedom but also control. You can drift as far as you want into your headspace and flesh out even your deepest pain without having it get to you. So, how do you do this exactly? Here's a set of guidelines to help you get started.

- Choose your material.

It is critical to select a material that complements your personality and situation. Keep three things in mind while you do so. First and foremost, it must be something you can envision yourself using—something that speaks to you. Don't pick materials you dislike or find intimidating, such as those that require largely technical skills to handle. Depending on the type of work you want to try, the resources you'll need can range from a single pencil to a whole set of sculpting and installation tools. There are no hard and fast rules. Choose the simplest and most accessible options. It makes no difference whether you recycle or buy. Second, the materials must fit within the confines of the current workstation. Depending on your circumstances, your workspace can range from your lap or a little spot on your bedroom floor to a complete workshop. Again, none of this is more important than determining which option is the most viable. Finally, the supplies must be something you don't mind discarding. When you're just starting out, the last thing you want to worry about is wasting expensive materials—unless, of course, you have enough resources and this doesn't concern you. Remember, the goal is not to create visually appealing or socially acceptable art but to hold space to free your genuine, spontaneous self.

- Don't wait to get started.

Don't wait for a mood to start. As soon as you have the time and the materials, just take them for grabs and go right into it. When you're new to art, the hardest part is usually getting started—that is practically normal—but don't let this stop you! Sometimes the pressure to do well can get in the way. Catch this before it builds up. Remind yourself that you are not in a competition and that your work will not be evaluated in any way. There will be no good or bad results, and you can choose not to show them to anyone. If despite convincing yourself you're still having trouble getting started, consider this tip: start with the smallest amount of the element your chosen art is composed of.

Take drawing, for example. Unless you've been doing this for some time, don't go right into recreating something that requires a lot of technical skill like a loved one's face. Start getting to know the feel of that drawing pencil in your hand, as you rest your eyes in the line you create. Draw a line. Then another, and another. Broken lines, continuous lines, thick and thin ones. Keep going. Just go on scribbling as you wish—you don't even have to try to build a form yet, but if you feel like it, go ahead. You can also experiment with different pressures on your pen or pencil, ranging from mild to forceful. Practice mindfulness as you experiment with different strokes, hues, and shapes. Notice how your mood and emotions shift moment by moment. Keep going until your hand movement feels more like an extension of your inner self. You can do something similar with painting, sculpture, or music.

• Be in the moment and enjoy yourself.

As you do this, resist the urge to think of something else. Pay attention to what is going on in the moment, even if it means simply rehearsing what is happening in your head. Notice every detail of the experience. Be able to identify what you like about it. In case a part of you seems to tell you that your work is not good, repeat to yourself that you are not looking to create something good, but something real–and real throws both good and bad in the mix. Let yourself become absorbed in the process. In some cases, you might just experience flow.

The Flow

Psychologists Mihaly Csikszentmihalyi and Jeanne Nakamura (2002) talked about a state of being "fully immersed in doing something you enjoy"—the flow state. Some people call it "being in the zone." When you are in this state, you don't worry about what to do next—you just let yourself go, spontaneously, unapologetically, and freely. According to Martins (2022), "If you're creating art, flow state is when you're so involved in the creation process that it's the only thing you're focused on." The keys are focus, concentration, spontaneity, and enjoyment. If you can get this going, it's an experience you'd surely want to be in from time to time. More often than not, it helps you become more attuned with your emotions and become more confident.

Look at the finished product and feel towards it.

When you are done, position your work so that you can freely gaze at it. Notice your thoughts, feelings, and physiological responses (your heartbeat, muscle tension, and breathing, among others). Use these questions to reflect on them.

- What do I think of my work?

- How do I feel about it?

- What part of me does this represent?

- How do I feel about that part?

- If that part can talk back, what would that part tell me, and how would I respond? Will we ever hit it off as friends?

- What is the role of this part in my life? Would it rather have a different role?

- Is there anything I'd like to thank this part of me for?

These questions will help you ponder things that let you connect to the parts of yourself you may have forgotten. Befriending the parts of ourselves we have once pushed away or otherwise forgotten paves the way to a harmonious inner self, where, more often than not, a lot of healing simply needs to take place.

Discover or Rediscover Hobbies

Use your time alone to try things you've never tried before or to pick up that last project you've left hanging in the garage. Revisit the things you used to enjoy but have almost forgotten. It doesn't have to be something huge either. It can be as simple as cooking a new meal, wearing your hair a different way, or trying out that new brand of aftershave. Nevertheless, you can also get a little more adventurous if you like. Make a bucket list of activities and document your experiences as you get to do each one. Try your hand at a beginner-friendly sport, do art, travel, or just be somewhere else (it doesn't have to be far), learn a new skill, find a side hustle you love, revisit old friends or relatives, pamper yourself, redefine your goals—the list is endless.

When you take the loneliness out of the word alone, your reality begins to transform. You begin to feel every bit of you, loosening slowly, gradually, as a budding rose. You begin to notice your heartbeat, and you begin to realize that your emotions aren't your enemies. You are a unified whole, and there's no need to split. There's no need to push back on the things about you that other people may not like. There's no reason to hide. You have every chance to be every bit who you are, and you can soak it all in all you want until you find the strength to go back and face the world, this time knowing there's a place inside you that says you can return to when you need it. When you take the loneliness out of the world alone, the pain subsides just a little bit so that it carries you out of a raging sea and into a quiet shore, where you could still watch the water but not get consumed.

Chapter 2

The Blues Ain't Nothing but a Mood Swing

"You are the one thing in the world, above all things, that you must never give up on." (Kingslover, 1988, p.232)

The Blues

Interest in depression has skyrocketed in the past decade (Wang et al., 2022). For instance, Google Trends revealed that, between 2010 and 2021, the number of people searching the word *depression* increased by 67%—and that's in the United States alone. It isn't surprising, considering the surge of recently diagnosed cases (Wang et al., 2017). As we speak, roughly 280 million people in the world experience depression (World Health Organization, 2021). That is a whopping 3.8% of the population—5.0% among adults and

5.7% among adults older than 60 years, statistics by the World Health Organization (2021) revealed. "It is the most common disorder in the United States," claim Wang and his colleagues (2022). Unfortunately, depression remains a vague term associated with a range of experiences, from an extremely low but normal mood drop to persistent manifestations of clinically significant symptoms. As the South African Applied College of Psychology (2017) has noted, "the word *depression* is a loose term for multiple diagnoses, each with a differing range of symptoms and treatments."

But what really is depression? To really answer this, let's first consider the mental health state mainly affected by depressive disorders: mood. Mood is an affective state. That is, it is closely related to our emotional experiences. It is, however, distinguished from emotions in that it tends to be more general than specific, and typically lasts longer than an emotion does. Everybody has a mood, and, like our emotions, this can fluctuate from high to low, often described as good or bad. A lot of things can trigger this—diet, exposure to sunlight, movement and exercise, and life events, including thoughts and emotions associated with these events, are the most recognized. Some personality traits can also predispose us to certain moods. For instance, the traits of agreeableness and openness are said to be significantly associated with cheerfulness and a generally positive mood (Komulainen et al., 2014). People tend to differ in terms of their mood stability. There are those who often maintain certain moods for longer periods of time, for instance, and then there are those who are prone to mood swings. Mood swings are described as a "sudden or intense change in emotional state (Leonard, 2020)." Undergoing life transitions, experiencing stress, an unhealthy diet, a lack of sleep, and the intake of medications that affect mood or sleep tend to influence these sudden shifts (Leonard, 2020). Under normal circumstances, mood can be improved by engaging in activities that spark our interest as well as those that tend to give us a pleasant or pleasurable experience. However, when it comes to mood disorders like depression and bipolar disorder, the scenario is entirely different. Barbara Kingslover, for instance, highlights this difference when she says:

"There is no point treating a depressed person as though she were just feeling sad, saying, 'There now, hang on, you'll get over it. Sadness is more or less like a head cold—with patience, it passes. Depression is like cancer." (Kingslover, 1988, p.232)

Some of those who battle with depression describe it as a sense of being stuck and unfeeling; others describe it as a seemingly endless loop of emotional turmoil with no end in sight. Among the toughest enemies? Hopelessness. Elizabeth Wurtzel goes on to say: "A human being can survive almost anything, as long as she sees the end in sight. But depression is so insidious, and it compounds daily, that it's impossible to ever see the end."

Often referred to as the blues, depression is a crippling mental health condition that can present itself in many ways. The Diagnostic and Statistical Manual of Mental Health Disorders dedicated two chapters to mood disorders, dividing them into two groups: (1) bipolar and related disorders and (2) depressive disorders. In a nutshell, bipolar disorders include occasional manic symptoms, while depressive disorders don't. Mania is characterized by grandiosity, risky behavior, agitation, flightiness, insomnia, distractibility, and excessive talkativeness—easily recalled using the acronym G.R.A.F.I.D.T.

On the other hand, depressive symptoms can include sleep disturbance, anhedonia (losing interest in previously pleasurable activities), concentration problems, excessive guilt, energy loss, psychomotor retardation, and suicidal tendencies—easily recalled using the acronym S.A.D.C.W.E.E.P.S. To get diagnosed, one has to meet specified criteria, including the required number of symptoms, the absence of confounding factors like medical conditions and substance abuse, and significant impairment in various areas of functioning. Clinically significant depressive episodes are classified as mild, moderate, or severe by ICD-10 and DSM-IV based on the number, kind, and severity of symptoms present, as well as the degree of functional impairment (National Institute for Health and Care Excellence, 2017).

What causes depression? The Center for Clinical Interventions (n.d.) claims that a variety of factors, including biological and psychological factors, contribute to depression.

Depression isn't *all in one's head*—it is neither hallucination or delusion nor imaginary. It affects our physical as well as emotional states, and it feeds on our sense of self-worth until we barely have any left. Psychological factors such as a habit of amplifying negatives, taking responsibility only for bad events, discounting the good, having rigid rules about how one should behave, and believing that you know what others are thinking and that they are thinking negatively of you, certainly don't help.

That said, battling depression is no easy feat. Sadly, when people around you lack this knowledge, they can easily discount or invalidate your experiences as something you can easily have control over. Advice like, "You just got to focus on the good stuff," for instance, although honestly well-meaning, more often than not, hurts a lot because having depression typically means recognizing the good stuff is not going to alter the state of your mood, no matter how hard you are trying to make them. Furthermore, the fact that things that usually help people feel better just don't work on you can be frustrating. Hence the popular quote: "Depression is like asthma: the presence of air is irrelevant to your inability to breathe."

For a person who experiences depression, the presence of good in their lives is irrelevant to the vacuum or turmoil brewing inside them. And the burden of explaining this to others can range from uncomfortable to overwhelming. And to most of us who've been in this boat, frustrating is largely an understatement. All this can be a huge blow to your already fickle self-esteem or those already overwhelming surges of guilt. Now, if you are experiencing some, if not all, of this, you might have wondered, at some point in time, "Will I ever get out?" Perhaps, you can no longer recall what it felt like to *not* have depression. Quite understandably, a part of you might just have given up trying to do so. Then again, another part might just be holding on with all its remaining strength, despite barely getting the acknowledgment it deserves for all its hard work keeping you afloat.

Take time to pause and acknowledge both parts. Let your tired part know you understand its struggles and frustrations. And that part of you that holds on? Go ahead and give it a long, tight hug. The rest of the world may attempt to rush your healing; after all, people generally aren't comfortable with each other's pain lest it reminds them of their own. Try not to listen. You are neither obliged to instantly see and grab hold of hope nor feel better right away. Healing takes time, and it is different for everybody—yes, even those who have a similar diagnosis. Mira Rothenberg, a remarkable psychologist, and author of the book Children with Emerald Eyes, talks about how she sees every individual as an intricate web that can only be unraveled by following its own unique pattern at just the right pace. I know it may not seem like it, but past the pain and hopelessness and past, all the burdens that kept you from tapping a huge chunk of your inner resources is a will to live, stronger than all doubt and fear. You won't be able to see it right now, but that's okay. Things continue to exist independent of our ability to sense them. Just give this thought a good look and then put it where you'll find it the moment that you're ready to take it in and believe it again—then remind yourself that for now, it's enough to just breathe.

The Turmoil

Our minds mostly consist of thoughts and feelings. While thoughts allow us to learn, recall, solve problems, decide, and generally make sense of everything around us and within us, emotions make the world go round. Feelings can draw our attention in a split second and prompt us into action just as fast. Unlike thoughts, though, our feelings communicate to us not through language but through body sensations or psychological responses associated with them. Feelings come at us from all directions—subtle, powerful, and mostly somewhat vague, or at least not as clear as thoughts are. Feelings leave so much room for interpretation, that it is often difficult to get the message—unless, of course, we learned to notice them, savor them, and master the art of bringing into awareness the sensations and messages they tell us about. Sometimes, feelings from the past come crashing through, catching us off guard. They can spring out what-ifs, could-have-been, and if-only too.

When we feel, our entire state is altered, though most of the time we are not mindful of this. A lot of us have this vague idea that emotions are all in our heads—that emotions aren't real, or at least, that they aren't real enough. So, the sensations and body reactions accompanying our emotions often come as a surprise, and whenever they get unpleasant, our natural tendency is always to recoil, to try to ignore, if not forget, them, and to not speak of them again if we can help it.

As we've mentioned earlier, we naturally stay away from whatever is painful. Recall that this is because pain is often a signal that something isn't right, and at the back of our heads, we know that anything of that sort can signal danger as well. That should be cool stuff except that the world has changed tremendously compared to when our complex brains first came to be. Life still has its set of dangers, but we've come quite far. Society has evolved so much that we no longer have to ordinarily hide from natural predators or freeze out in the cold. We don't need emotions the way our kind used to, centuries ago. In fact, acting on emotions alone can have serious drawbacks. But all this doesn't change the way our entire nervous system is wired. A huge part of who we are, for instance, is still vigilant about these threats, whether or not they're existent. So, it makes sense why we'd rather steer clear of anger, fear, or regret, though no matter how we try, we can only blot them out for a time. We can't really run away.

Remarkably, we are also studded with resilience. Except for that, not a lot of us are aware of it. You see, the tougher life is in our memory, the more vigilant we become, and the more we are kept from seeing ourselves past our burdened should-haves and what-ifs. For centuries, human beings have been discovering and rediscovering secrets to getting past this, but despite the endless writing of books and postings of web articles, we can still very easily miss it all. Perhaps, it is simply because, more often than not, deep wisdom comes with experience, and experience requires us to venture out or into ourselves—both of which can expose us to anticipated threats, as we don't like to feel vulnerable. When we've been caught in the middle of hopelessness and fear for so long, we also lose the courage to venture out. Although we still can. Only that, this isn't easy. More often than not, it involves resisting our natural human instinct to go with our gut and act on impulse. It takes courage to experience hurt and potential discomfort. We all wanted to maximize our ability to think, but not all of us were willing to chart unknown waters. Nevertheless, we can still try. A lot of us had, sometimes gaining profound knowledge out of the experience; other times, simply making sense of the whys—which can be just as powerful as the first.

What about loneliness? Where does it fall in the grand scheme of things? If there are no bad emotions, why does it feel so wrong? Well, this book can tell you, but the insight you've gained won't be as raw and precious as it would be when, instead of hearing others, you learn to listen as your loneliness speaks. While you're at it, you might try this simple exercise:

Imagine your loneliness, The Emotion, as a person trying to tell you something but being ignored or pushed back. Now imagine your thoughts, The Thought, as another person, talking to loneliness. What do you think the exchanges between them are like? What does The Thought say to The Emotion? Is it critical? Judging? Invalidating? We wouldn't do this to another person; why are we doing this to ourselves? Now take a moment to relish that tiny bit of wisdom right there.

Our thoughts are keys to our emotions, and our emotions are doors to our thoughts. We have to realize that both of these aren't facts—they are a mixture of a lot of data, truth, and lies included. Just because something makes sense does not mean it is logical. It's like a delicate web. On the surface, it looks just like every other web, containing all its elements. But if you just zoom in, you'd see every web is intricately different. This is also why, despite making good connections with other people, we can still be lonely. You see, bridges only connect certain parts of two islands, and even then, it's not a guarantee that travelers will be able to explore every inch of both, and that is okay.

They say no man is an island—that is just false. In fact, we are all islands, interconnected by bridges of many kinds. Sometimes our bridges are feeble; sometimes our bridges are rocks. Some bridges are made of flowers; others are made of twigs. In this light, every relationship is different, and the absence of a bridge in one area is not always permanent. Sometimes, we just have to wait for the low tide to stop working, or when the wind is just right. Other times we just have to acquire the right tools, so we can build another bridge amidst a raging storm. Emotions are like water around the

30

islands. Sometimes all it does is mess with the bridges we create—other times it gets to us.

So how do we deal with these waters? There are zillions of effective ways, but not all are right for you. When you understand this, you will also wake up to the realization that, when a strategy, a suggestion, or even professional advice, doesn't work in your situation, it isn't something personal. It isn't because something is wrong with you, or something is wrong with the tool. It's just that, you can't force a nail where a shoe should have been. In the next chapters, we are going to check out strategies that have worked for a lot of people, and more often than not, these are things with great potential to work for you too. Nevertheless, allow yourself to explore the new insights you might gain from them, and tailor-fit these to your situation. Don't be afraid to seek professional help when needed, and do not be ashamed to admit when one approach is not helping.

How to Deal With the Blues and the Turmoil

Finding the right tool sometimes happens in a snap; other times, it requires days, months, or even years of searching. Don't give up, and keep learning. Every bit of information can be used to your advantage if you allow it to. As for how to do this, here are a few steps:

First, increase your knowledge of available resources. Keep checking out the available resources—what are they? Who offers them? Do they cost anything? Are there pros and cons? How are they likely going to help me?

Second, explore your attitude toward these resources. Reflect on them, sense how you feel towards them, and explore your apprehensions and hopes. Remember, you will not be able to use a tool without realizing it exists, and you will not use a tool until you believe it works either.

Third, identify the prerequisites. Certain resources require that you have the skills to use them. If this is the case, begin working on these skills first as soon as you can.

Finally, keep in mind that failure is a building block, not a stumbling block. When we see failures as stumbling blocks, it hampers our self-efficacy or faith in what we can do. When this happens, it dampens our resolve. When we change our perception of failure, however, and see it as a thing to build on or build with, we do just that—we use it to our advantage; we make it work for us, instead of against us. This way, we minimize the possibility of demotivating ourselves and maximize our chances of succeeding.

To sum it up, as you go on exploring and trying things out, think of these things: knowledge, faith, and skill. Know what is available, have faith in its power to help, and build the skills needed to use it right—and as you set out to apply them, don't give up and be prepared to rock.

Available Psychotherapies

For starters, should you feel the need to seek professional help, here are currently available psychotherapeutic techniques that might just be what you need to overcome the inner turmoil of negative emotions, as well as the thoughts and beliefs that often lurk beneath the surface.

Cognitive Behavioral Therapy (CBT)

CBT is among the most widely used and most extensively researched of all psychotherapies. It rests on the premise that much of our emotional distress comes from negative and self-defeating automatic thoughts. An automatic thought is loosely defined as the first thing that comes to your mind after encountering a significant event or after becoming conscious of another automatic thought. This is typically an assumption; an attempt to describe or define what is happening or make sense of the situation. It can also be an attempt to predict an outcome. Automatic thoughts can be positive or negative, but negative ones often cause us the most distress. Some people are said to be more susceptible to negative automatic thoughts than others. Past experiences, as well as physical or physiological vulnerabilities, can influence these thoughts. Without our awareness of them, these thoughts can creep into our consciousness so subtly that we often end up only recognizing the emotion they elicit. As a result, we blame the event for causing the emotion and forget about checking the validity of the thought altogether.

Extremely negative or self-defeating thoughts usually come from what psychologists refer to as cognitive biases—these patterns of coming up with conclusions that often disregard salient information about the situation, resulting in conclusions that, without getting the chance to be validated by opposing or disagreeing information, are typically not founded on evidence. In cognitive behavior therapy, therapists teach their clients about the most common cognitive distortions and guide them toward exploring their current thoughts and beliefs about a significant event, initially thought to have caused the current distress. Cognitive behavior therapy focuses on the present and, while it does explore a bit of the past, does not dwell on things that already happened any more than it does in trying to teach the client to catch maladaptive thoughts early, change faulty thinking, and alleviate emotional distress coming from those (Austad, 2009).

Dialectical Behavior Therapy

Closely related to cognitive behavior therapy, dialectical behavior therapy also agrees that thoughts influence a lot of how we feel. Initially designed for individuals who feel their emotions more intensely than others, it rests on the premise that two opposite things could be true at the same time, encouraging clients to become comfortable with ambivalence and empowering them to work through positive growth while experiencing turmoil. It emphasized recognizing and accepting all emotions, including the extremely unpleasant, painful, or even initially menacing ones. It makes use of mindfulness strategies and focuses on helping clients direct their attention toward the present moment instead of regretting the past or constantly ruminating about the future. It encourages interpersonal effectiveness by providing clients with specific interpersonal response patterns (Delray Center for Healing, n.d.). And of course, it aims to help clients acquire and level up their emotion regulation skills, which may include labeling and recognizing feelings, finding barriers to transforming emotions, increasing pleasant emotional experiences, raising attentiveness to current emotions, doing the opposite action, and using distress tolerance strategies (Delray Center for Healing, n.d.).

Gestalt Therapy

"Gestalt therapy is a form of psychotherapy that is centered on increasing a person's awareness, freedom, and self-direction. It's a form of therapy that focuses on the present moment rather than past experiences," says Brennan (2021) of WebMD. It rests on the premise of holism, or the idea that we are an intimate interconnection of our various parts and that the totality of who we are is our true essence, greater than fragments of ourselves. It aims to help people increase their moment-to-moment awareness, self-direction, and freedom.

According to this principle, we are all seeking a sense of balance in our lives, and this is achieved whenever we get to meet a need that becomes the object of our perception at the moment. However, our strategies of getting what we need from the world or of dealing with the current stresses of our environment can become ineffective at some point, resulting in an unmet need that eventually fades into the background as we focus our attention on the new need that comes forth in the moment. It is only a matter of time, however, before these unmet needs resurface and get in the way of our ability to cope with the present demands of our environment, creating further distress. Like dialectical behavior therapy, Gestalt therapy also helps clients work towards accepting their unpleasant emotions by being present and aware of these experiences (Brennan, 2021).

Interpersonal Family Systems

The internal family system rests on the premise that we all have parts, or normal subpersonalities, that are distinct with their own characteristics, wounds, burdens, and untapped potentials. Whenever a person encounters a significantly distressing or traumatic event, parts of themselves take on roles that can obscure their true potential and trigger the other parts to become indifferent, resentful, or fearful toward them—so much so that these parts become "exiled." On the other hand, as a response to these, other parts can also take on other roles, such as the manager role or the firefighter role, among others. Managers are "protective parts that function to control people's surroundings and manage emotions and tasks to navigate daily life," while firefighters "prevent attempts to prevent exiles from overwhelming the self by bringing painful or threatening emotions into consciousness," says Psychology Today (2022). Furthermore, one hallmark of this therapeutic approach is that it does not pigeonhole individuals into their diagnoses. As its proponent Richard Schwartz would say, "The big insight was that giving a troubled person a psychiatric diagnosis and seeing that as the sole or main cause of their symptoms was unnecessarily limiting, pathologizing, and could become self-reinforcing (Schwartz, 2021)." The process involves fleshing out the parts, or differentiating oneself from them, feeling towards the parts, exploring what each part might fear about the other, and ultimately unburdening (Aaron-Wayne, 2023).

Things You Can Try On Your Own

Based on a combination of techniques employed by these psychotherapies, on the other hand, these are strategies you may want to try out on your own. If you have an existing mental health diagnosis, however, please be sure to ask your doctor or therapist about it. Also, these suggestions are in no way a replacement for the more extensive, guided approach of their source therapies.

1. Be present and aware.

2. Differentiate yourself from your thoughts and emotions.

3. Notice how your emotions feel physically and sit with the feeling.

4. Identify and name the emotion or emotions involved—or name them yourself.

5. Be aware of how you feel about the emotion, and ask yourself what you are afraid of if you allow yourself to feel it.

6. Explore your thoughts and check for rigidity or overgeneralization—cognitive biases often leave no room for explanations that contradict the first thought.

7. Identify cognitive biases and name them if you can.

8. Challenge these biases by acquiring more information about their premise. Look for evidence-based information and put your intuition on pause.

9. Notice when you are being critical or unkind to yourself. Change the self-defeating thought into a

more realistic one.

10. Practice accepting the parts of yourself you feel compelled to push away.

11. Trust yourself; it may not look like it, but you are doing the best you can, given the information available to you.

12. Cultivate a growth mindset and use this to your advantage.

13. Aim for the smallest win.

14. Celebrate the smallest wins.

15. Pause if you must, but keep going.

16. Remember that learning doesn't stop, and neither should you.

Dealing with emotional turmoil is no easy task—Some days you might just feel like giving up. It's usually difficult to find people who understand what you are going through—this can be frustrating. Plus, although a lot of the tips you've just read may appear quite simple at a glance, they may be easier said than done. Don't give up! Keep reminding yourself that you're not having it easy, and don't force yourself to do everything at once. You can try out one thing at a time and see what works for you. Sometimes progress feels slow—don't let this fool you into giving up. Life is not a race, and every moment belongs to you, so let yourself breathe.

Chapter 3

The Cloudy Days

"There's a crack in everything. That's how life gets in." (Kingslover, 1988, p.232)

H ow do you find the rain? Do you like the melancholy it brings with it, as some do? Do you like the way it sort of dims the world and sends birds and butterflies into hiding? Or, are you among those who, at the sight of big, fat rainclouds, unconsciously bite their lips in annoyance or give off that subtle, "not-again" sigh? People have mixed feelings about storms and rain, but most would agree with one thing: nobody wants to get caught in a downpour—except maybe that handful of kids who most likely couldn't think of anything more fun.

Have you ever gaped in wonder at children playing in the rain? They aren't at all different from us–their hair, clothes, and faces get drenched as much as ours would; they'd shiver from the cold as we would have; they'd catch a cold, any day, for failing to dry themselves up after being outdoors in that weather. Yet the glint in their eyes and grins on their faces are unmistakable as they run around unconcerned. They aren't letting minor inconveniences get in the way of living life. We have a lot to relearn from little kids.

<hr />

Finding a Silver Lining

When was the last time you appreciated the silver linings in those big, old gray nimbus clouds? Chances are, you haven't, just like any of us. Despite it being the subject of poets, musicians, and other creatives for so long, we don't normally go searching for silver linings every time we're caught in bad weather. We fix our attention on the rain, on the overall gray atmosphere, or on its inconveniences. We don't go cloud watching either, nor do we save perhaps a quick glance for some practical reason, like checking how bad it is. Now that we've mentioned it, it's actually worth pondering upon.

You see, our brains literally don't pick up a lot of background information, if any at all. Its first response is to filter these out and zoom into our object of focus from the get-go. Simply put, although we're capable of sensing anything and everything within our sensory threshold, we normally filter much of it out, often unconsciously. Missing a lot of the things we don't pay attention to, including those right under our noses, makes a lot of sense in this light.

We usually get it—this is our mind's way of preventing sensory overload—and with a reasonable cause! But then, on the other hand, this can keep us from noticing the good stuff during difficult times—where the threat or potential cause of our distress automatically becomes the primary object of our attention—even when the slightest bit of hope would have helped. This explains why it's hard to catch a glimpse of good in times of heightened stress—it requires a conscious shift of focus away from the bad stuff, something our minds are probably already so good at this point. Plus, replacing something easy and familiar with anything hard and new—at least in the beginning–quite frequently, can be downright daunting. So, next time somebody tells you this should be easy, don't let that invalidate your experience. Acknowledge how this doesn't come naturally, then work on building a habit that allows you to do it more deliberately, more effectively, and more consistently.

Finding a silver lining can develop our ability to appreciate life in the midst of troubles or challenges. It encourages us to suspend judgment about whether or not our entire life is good and helps us avoid stressing over concerns that are born out of limited information, or, worse, baseless assumptions and random irrational thoughts. It reminds us that, no matter how bad things are on one end, it doesn't necessarily reflect our entire situation. Things can be difficult and not necessarily awful. Life could be hard and yet still worth living. Reality is a thing that exists on its own—with or without us noticing. We can lose sight of something without really losing it, and the things we sense moment by moment, along with all memories and hopes, are no greater than the totality of the continuum on which we live. Dark clouds can be menacing. They don't only alert us of an impending storm—that is, if it isn't lashing out already—they also blot out the sun, and pretty much of the sky too. We have to look for silver linings to remind us that, despite how it looks from where we stand, the sun shines and the sky's still blue. Clouds don't change the color of the sky, just our perception of it. In due time the clouds will clear, and much of your gray-cloaked world will come out light and refreshed.

Chapter 4

Laughing in the Face of Loneliness

"A good laugh heals a lot of hurts." (Kingslover, 1988, p.232)

W hen was the last time you heard yourself laugh? And I don't mean one of those brief, tight laughs you get to force out of your mouth to ward off awkward situations, or those fake, hollow ones you let out to convince others you're less stressed than you actually are. I was referring to those spontaneous, joyous offshoots. Do you remember what it's like? To really laugh—to feel that first hint of laughter rumbling in your stomach, that builds up in seconds into a bubbling stream, eventually escaping from you, taking all the negatives with it, and replacing them with that nice and warm aftermath? To feel your muscles quiver in a good way, as the world lights up, just for a moment, and everything that has ever worried you suspended in midair? A laugh like that—it's just full bliss. When was the last time you'd let yourself slip into one?

Children laugh at almost everything—when they are nervous, when they make a mistake, when they are unsure—and it doesn't only help them diffuse tension. It transforms the atmosphere around them as well. They laugh as if they'd never had that huge tantrum an hour before, as if they'd never had their knees scraped or their hearts broken. They laugh shamelessly, gleefully, and their laughter is contagious. They knew nothing of stifling a laugh or holding back tears, and this simply lets them go all out, replenishing each moment with experience after experience—emotion after emotion. How most of us admire—even secretly envy them! According to a web article by New York Post (n.d.), one OnePoll study suggested that those who regarded themselves as spontaneous were also 40% more likely to consider themselves happy. The older we get, however, the less spontaneous we tend to become (Lumley, 2022).

We, too, were spontaneous as children, life coach Naomi Light (n.d.) observes. "We have routines, but we also have imagination; time is a mystery, and we are always seeking the unknown. This enables us to truly explore the world," she recalls. "As adults, however, we have everything planned. We think we know what to expect from the world around us, how we 'should' respond to events, and how we feel about projected outcomes and opportunities." Robinson and his colleagues (2018) made similar observations: "While we used to slip in and out of laughter spontaneously as children, we tend to diminish this ability when we grow older." Unfortunately, the more we constrain ourselves, the less we also laugh. Is this simply a case of growing up? Or the *yang* side of the blessing, knowing more than twice as much as we did when we were small? Then again, maybe we're just forgetting that we can still be our true selves and that it's okay to be our true selves. It's okay to play and be silly, and it's okay to laugh and cry at will. Just like Antoine de Saint-Exupéry had put it in that beloved classic, *Little Prince*: "Growing up is not a problem—forgetting is."

Humor as a Positive Coping Strategy

According to Scott (2022), humor can "build resilience to stress, as well as improve overall physical and emotional health." It helps us bond with the people around us, strengthening the quality of our relationships, for one, aside from lifting up some of the negatives. She calls it a healthy and effective coping mechanism and says that, though humor may not come naturally to some of us, it can be developed with a change of perspective and "a bit of practice." But how do we find humor in difficult situations, exactly? While there is a myriad of other ways to find something funny, the role of these three should certainly not be overlooked: honesty, absurdity, and exaggeration. That is, when something is incredibly, unapologetically honest, and ridiculously unreasonable at the same time, it becomes funny.

To develop your sense of humor further, Scott recommends four quite obvious, but often overlooked, things: to start with a smile, to take a step back, to value the extremes, and to hang around with people who have quite a good sense of humor themselves—oh, and who would forget watching funny movies and video clips—or any sort of entertainment, for that matter, memes included? The thing is, we eventually learn to adapt to things we consistently expose ourselves to, whether or not we make a conscious effort. Of course, deliberately doing what you can to speed up the process is quite advantageous. Take Scott's second advice, for example: taking a step back. Here you consciously try to view your situation as an outsider instead of someone actually in it (e.g., what would you say to a person experiencing the same thing?) and then look for the absurdity in it. Sometimes stuff just comes out as funny on its own, popping out like a tiny bit of sunshine, that all you really have to do is notice it and take it for the grabs. Other times we need to look for it ourselves, and it may sometimes feel like having to sift tiny diamonds from a heap of sand. The more we do that, however, the less effort we'd need in the future to spot them.

Healing Through Laughter
How to Laugh in the Face of Loneliness.

No doubt, laughter feels good, but its benefits go beyond that. The phrase "laughter is the best medicine," became cliche for a reason. According to Robinson and his colleagues (n.d.), the benefits of laughter range from helping us boost mood to actually strengthening our immune system.

Change your mind about laughing alone.
We are so used to laughing with others that laughing alone—much less in the midst of unpleasant emotions like loneliness—may seem odd, or awkward, if not almost taboo. Changing your mind about laughing in these conditions helps release you from unnecessary constraints and allows you to just slip into the process whenever you want. To do this, try to picture yourself laughing alone or laughing when you're close to tears. Now notice how you feel toward this mental image. Next, notice the thoughts that pop up. Write them down if necessary. You are likely going to get a few phrases, revealing just why laughing on your own and in the midst of a difficult situation does not appeal to you. Once you've caught the thought, study it. Is it a valid, rational thought? Check out what science says, and decide from there whether or not it is worth changing. Once you have done this, you can either go ahead and actively seek out things to laugh about or proceed to the next suggestion.

Once you've decided to subject yourself to environmental conditions that are likely going to help you laugh, you may want to try these steps: First, identify what usually made you laugh in the past. It can be a movie, a memory, a person—anything, really. Next, determine if it is safe, and then try to think of the best way to gain access to these. Finally, get into that place and allow yourself to smile. Let it guide you into soft laughter, and allow it to build when it does. Now, this may make you feel quite silly at first; remind yourself that it's practically normal. Also, these suggestions are not the only way to do it, so don't hesitate to get creative. Furthermore, don't worry if you can't figure out what they are right away. You're not the only one either. According to Sobato (2019), for instance, even scientists struggle to explain exactly what makes people laugh. This is despite the fact that "almost everyone understands intuitively what humor is." When it comes to the benefits of laughter, the reason why we are laughing is of little importance. It turns out, the effect of laughter doesn't just soothe the psyche—it relaxes our body as well, benefiting it generously.

Laugh at will using laughter yoga techniques.
Daidson (2021) describes laughter yoga as "a popular movement and breathing exercise that aims to cultivate joy, bring out your inner child, and help you let go of daily life stressors." According to Greene (2020), laughter has the ability to change our lives. To maximize this potential, one has to learn to laugh at will. As a laughter yoga therapist, Greene attests that this is possible both in the presence of others and when alone. Laughter, according to her, is an aerobic exercise.

Although widely known to naturally be triggered by joy, fun, and other pleasant emotions alone, the process can be flipped. That is, you can consciously choose to laugh to be happier, not the other way around.

To obtain the same benefits as spontaneous laughter, she encourages her readers to laugh from the diaphragm. This can be done by relaxing the jaw and letting the mouth hang slightly open. Greene also suggested steering clear of tight clothing, especially wrapping around the belly area. Deliberate laughing is best done for a ten to fifteen minutes duration, ideally in the morning. Celeste also outlined various lighter yoga exercises namely: laughter sounds; aloha laughter; very good, very good, YAY!; gibberish talk; and household chores laughter, among others. Let's take a quick look at these descriptions for each:

- **Laughter sounds:** This is simply making laughing sounds when you don't feel like laughing until finally, real laughter kicks in.

- **Aloha Laughter:** This involves raising both arms upwards saying "alo…" for quite a bit (without breaking your breath) and ending up with "Ha! Hahahaha!" until you start laughing.

- **Very good, very good, YAY!:** For this exercise, clap twice, say very good twice, and then exclaim a happy

"Yay!" allowing your inner child to take over.

- **Gibberish Talk:** This is exactly as the title implies! Just try speaking in a made-up language and pretend to have a really funny conversation with somebody. You can get hand gestures and facial expressions involved too. Do this until you are really laughing.

- **Household Chores Laughter:** Let's play pretend for this one. Imagine you are cleaning the house and laughing all the way!

Greene believes that laughing is like a muscle. It's going to be awkward and maybe even difficult at first, but you become better at it over time—then it gets easier.

———◆———

Welcome your inner child and cultivate playfulness.

Think of that famous line by George Bernard Shaw: "We do not stop playing because we grow old. We grow old because we stop playing." According to Robinson (n.d.), play isn't for children alone—it is beneficial for adults as well. Play provides us with stimulation as well as helps us get into a more relaxed state. It further allows us to connect to the people around us, have that much-needed break from the hustle and bustle of everyday life, and generate fun, which, according to William

Glasser (2014), is one of our primary needs and—contrary to popular opinion—definitely not something we could simply shrug off or deem unimportant.

And if all that wasn't enough, play is also said to boost one's creativity and foster a positive mental attitude. As a web article by Well Life Family Medicine (n.d.) would put it: "When you play with the problem, you can often transform it into an opportunity for creative learning." This is likely because our attitude towards a problem alters the level of negative emotions associated with it, dramatically decreasing them; and since intense emotions typically get in the way of clear thinking, this allows us to tap our creative and problem-solving potential more easily.

Take note, however, that playfulness isn't minimizing the seriousness of our concerns, or denying the threats before us. Rather, it is maintaining the ability to still allow oneself to have fun in the midst of all those. It is the lighthearted approach to life that makes us playful; children are playful not because they close their eyes or are never afraid. In fact, it might just be the opposite of that—they see the world wide-eyed, so even when some things are too scary or sad, they still get to spot the good stuff.

But how do you let out your inner child and cultivate playfulness? The first step is admitting that it's there, recognizing that this part of you is valuable, and that it's perfectly okay and safe to nurture it. You see, while our inner child can be playful, spontaneous, and creative, we may also associate it with the stuff about ourselves we like the least—like the tendency to appear soft and gullible instead of impenetrable and strong. More often than not, especially when we've experienced a lot of earlier trauma, acknowledging this part of us might just leave us feeling vulnerable—and we don't like that. Once we've gotten past this, however, it becomes a lot easier for us to let ourselves go. The second step is to get comfortable being in this state and make a little more room for it in our lives. This can range from finally entertaining the idea of actually doing something fun—regardless of people's opinions—to actually breaking character, such as being all goofy and boisterous, for instance, when you're used to being serious and contained. Of course, it's okay to test the waters first. Some would take this to a whole new level and go on vacation elsewhere, for instance, unleashing their spontaneous selves in places where no one really knows them—you wouldn't want to break character in the middle of a corporate meeting. It doesn't always have to be something this big, however. More often than not, learning a new sport, spending time with your friend's or relative's kids, taking on babysitting jobs, running with your dog—or volunteering to take someone else's dog, if you don't have one—learning to paint with brighter colors, among a gazillion other things, might just do the trick.

Rekindling Positivity

There's probably nothing harder than staying positive in the midst of depression. Think of breathing easily in the middle of an asthma attack—you can probably do it, but not without labor and, in most cases, not without help.

Fortunately, according to Smith (2023), positivity in the midst of depression, while difficult, is quite possible. He went on as far as to say that depression doesn't only happen to people with difficult childhoods and pessimists—in unlikely times, it can strike any positive, happy individual who grew up in loving homes just as much. As Smith put it, "By committing yourself to a healing journey, you can approach positivity for depression one small step at a time and eventually reap the rewards." That is, there are things you can do on your end to help yourself, and these don't have to be huge things either. After all, all it takes is a tiny flicker to start a fire that could consume acres of vegetation in a gulp.

The Real Deal About Staying Positive

Fredrickson (2013) defines positivity as the experience of pleasant emotions—gratitude, serenity, and love, among others. These emotions help us broaden our awareness, build our strengths, and strive to improve ourselves. Thus, they pave the way for transformation every time we experience them

(Frederickson, 2013). It's no surprise, then, that people seek out positivity in their lives. Generally, positivity is known to have a wide array of benefits. For one, Mayo Clinic (n.d.) noted a number of its health benefits: from better mood and reduced risk of certain illnesses to better psychological and physical well-being and increased lifespan. While there is no single, clear-cut explanation for why this is so at the moment, a lot of theories point toward how positivity helps individuals effectively deal with stressful situations.

Interestingly though, Fredrickson also noted that while positivity can be deep, natural, spontaneous, and harmonious, it can also be superficial, artificial, insincere, and obsessive. While the former has considerable benefits, the latter may actually backfire—encouraging one to outwardly deny all things negative, for instance, which can be detrimental to one's mental health. Simply put, not all attempts to remain positive are helpful. While it seems logical to think of positivity as an attempt to direct one's attention to positive thoughts and experiences alone, Stewart (2023) reminds us that "healthy positivity isn't 100% positive." In her coaching blog, *How to Distinguish Healthy Positivity from Toxic Positivity,* she mentioned how healthy positivity brings forth "subtle feelings such as open-mindedness, curiosity, empathy, contentment, optimism, generosity, harmony, kindness, compassion, wisdom, perseverance, flexibility, and belief in others" more often than it does notable bouts of feel-good highs.

Stewart also noted that when we begin to take our desire to stay positive to an extreme, requiring ourselves and those around us to eliminate all traces of negativity, it becomes toxic. It is just as Wilding (2021) discussed in another blog: "Healthy positivity becomes toxic when it denies, minimizes, or invalidates a person's emotions." Healthy positivity is being 70–90% positive, Stewart went on to say. That said, you might have to make a mental note to never trust superlatives. Rather than perfect, go for what's real.

If you've ever been around people who unwittingly insist on this half-baked version of positivity, you probably know how emotionally draining and invalidating it is. That said, you can let out that breath you are holding, and rest assured that we won't be doing that here. You are not obliged to feel positive about your situation and don't force yourself onto the positivity train until you're ready. There are, however, a few things you can try to build a less negative outlook while allowing yourself to acknowledge your difficult experiences and all the unpleasant emotions that come with them. Think of a calm horizon at dawn or dusk—pretty, isn't it? The mingling of light and dark in twilight exudes such depth and color. It is okay to see both dark and light in life. If you let yourself, you might just get a glimpse of—or even a real good look at—how beautiful life can still be despite everything. You won't be able to see it by staring at a lightbulb. Be sure to go for the real deal!

Getting to Know the Subtle Game Changers: Gratitude and Serenity

As said, healthy positivity can manifest itself as one of many pleasant emotions. Let's focus on two of them: gratitude and serenity.

Gratitude

Loosely defined as appreciation for the good things, Chowdhury (2019) sees gratitude as "acknowledging the good things in life". Jans-Bekens et al defines it as "a sense of happiness in response to something good," and The Merriam-Webster's Dictionary simply translates it as thankfulness. We can think of it, therefore, as the ability to name the good stuff and appreciate it. That, in itself, has many benefits. Logan (2022) pointed out that "feeling thankful can improve sleep, mood, and immunity." Russell & Fosha (2008) also believed that gratitude has a healing effect. For example, in a 2017 article on psychology.com, Ackerman (2017) was able to identify more than 28 research findings on how gratitude actually helps.

Unfortunately, it is not easy to feel grateful in the midst of loneliness or depression. More often than not, when negative emotions are intense or when your mood is particularly low, it is quite difficult to shift your focus toward the good things.

This is normal. Believing that there is indeed nothing good going on with your life right now or that, if there is, you no longer care is also quite common. Luckily, this doesn't mean that you cannot plant the seed of gratitude or do something to cultivate your inner environment for it to grow. You see, a lot of people find it hard to be grateful because they are looking for a feel-good state instead of an action. But then, you cannot get into this feel-good state unless you engage in the practice. So, this time, try not to aim for the results—allow yourself to break down the strategy into super small bits and focus on those instead. The rest will follow. To do this, here are a few tips:

1. Define or redefine good.

If gratitude is the appreciation of good things, it makes sense to be able to tell what good things are first. Coming up with a realistic and measurable definition of good can help you manage your expectations and look for things that can actually be present in your life. While the answer to the question "What is good?" has sparked a long-standing philosophical debate for centuries—that is, humans have been trying to answer this for so long and still are currently—we can classify the idea into two categories. One, as (1) something worth having to enhance life, and (2) as something morally obligatory. For starters, ditch the second idea and focus on the first.

This is because while the former has a lot to do with your personal experience, the latter is largely based on what is agreed upon by other people, which may or may not match your unique situation and perspective. That said, it's not going to help you improve your ability to be grateful at the moment because more often than not, these can have little to no connection to what truly matters to you.

Aside from this, there is no way we can really control other people's outlook. William Glasser (2014) believes that one of the paths to finding happiness is focusing on the things we can control, rather than worrying about those we could not. This thought also echoes the beliefs of ancient Stoic Philosophies, which emphasized the value of focusing on things that are up to us, rather than wasting our efforts on those we can't possibly do anything about on our end (Irvine, 2009).

When defining what you consider good, therefore, try to separate it from what is right in the eyes of other people. This is not your concern. Rather, ask yourself what about the things you truly want—explore your idea of a good life honestly and shamelessly and be able to draw inspiration from there. Next, think of what contributes to it, even if it's just one percent of the good. This *good* doesn't have to be huge or profound—it can be small conveniences. And it's okay to stay away from the cliche.

2. Look for the almost-good.

If you've been gravitating towards the negatives for some time now, chances are, identifying the good won't be a breeze. So, instead of forcing yourself to *see the sun,* allow yourself to celebrate the slightest gaps in your cloudy sky—the tiniest glimpse of blue or gray. You don't have to feel good about it. Just N.O.T.I.C.E.—that is, (N) note it, (O) observe it, (T) take it, (I) imprint it, (C) celebrate it, and (E) encourage yourself to see more.

3. Continue to heighten your awareness.
As we've been mentioning throughout the book, always make it a point to look for the next best thing. Allow yourself to keep noticing, and just sit with the awareness that these tiny good things are poking their heads into your difficult situation. Resist the urge to make promises to yourself such as telling yourself that you will soon experience more of this. Just be in the moment.

4. Don't use your mood or feeling as a gauge for success.
In fact, don't think about success or failure. Just keep noticing the good and your body's response to it. Feel the bitterness dissolve into its gentler cousin, sadness. Allow yourself to sigh or smile in response. Close your eyes if it helps. Let a tear fall to release some of the anger. Acknowledge that your situation is hard. Now imagine the tiny fragments of good clearing-up space in the corner: a very small space that may not grow as fast as you want but a clear sky nonetheless.

5. Be able to do this for at least a few minutes every day.

You will know when gratitude is beginning to sprout because there will be subtle shifts in your entire system which, though not necessarily enough to count as "feeling good" again, do alleviate some of the weight or tension you've been in for some time now.

Serenity

Most of us would automatically associate serenity with tranquility, or a sense of calm or peace, but while it does bring about these two, it's not just that. According to Arnout (2019), "Pejner defined Serenity as an emotional experience that contributes to the acceptance of a situation." He himself describes it as a state of "physical, mental, emotional and spiritual homeostasis when life conditions can be managed or accepted." Simply put, we can associate serenity with three words: acceptance, balance, and peace. Just like gratitude and positivity in general, serenity isn't easy to come by in the midst of depression. When attained, however, it is a powerful game changer.

According to Huzler (n.d.), serenity can be cultivated through concentration. When we focus on things that truly matter to us, we release ourselves from the worries attached to things that are less significant. Ironically, if we strip ourselves of all the unnecessary burdens we have accumulated throughout life, we'd realize that the things that weigh us down most, aren't the things we care more deeply about, but rather, the things the rest of the world tell us we should be directing our efforts on. Interestingly, the more we get to identify what these things are and eliminate them from the equation whenever we have to make vital decisions or assess the quality of our lives—which, by the way, we tend to periodically do—our amount of distress also becomes significantly less.

Serenity Meditation

Despite dating back to ancient times, meditation is slowly regaining popularity in the modern world. It basically involves three essential things:

1. *Attention.* Attention is simply focusing on one thing to the exclusion of all others (McCallum, n.d.). This is particularly important in serenity meditation because it not only allows us to connect to our environment and our inner experience but also makes it possible for us to eliminate distractions. As pioneer psychologist William James (1890) put it, "What we attend to becomes our reality" (Austad, 2009).

2. *Imagination.* If attention allows us to be in tune with sensory and inner experiences, imagination helps us form mental images of things that we cannot see, smell, taste, or hear. Timalsina (2020) calls it a tool to "enrich our experience." When used along with mindfulness, imagination is a powerful tool to help us focus and relax.

3. *Focus.* Focus is our ability to maintain our attention. It allows us to concentrate on what matters to us in our moment-to-moment awareness. According to Huxter (n.d.), "A main feature of serenity meditation is the development of focused attention—Samadhi—gathered and placed on a single object."

With these three in mind, check out these simple steps:

1. Find a good place.

Begin by choosing a time and place that allows you to be in full concentration. You don't have to be in a breathtaking landscape or anything (although that's nice too)—just look for somewhere safe where you are less likely to get interrupted.

2. Eliminate distractions.

Distractions can be anything from the external environment, such as clutter, or anything from within, such as thoughts and emotions—particularly those connected to the past (such as regrets) and the future (such as worries). Allow yourself to put them on a shelf somewhere before beginning. You can do this by consciously resisting the urge to attend to them. You may even verbally express this intention to yourself before you begin.

3. Choose an object of attention.

Just like potential distractions, your object of attention can be anything from the environment or from within you. Scott (2021) of Very Well Mind suggests it is best to start with just your breath, but you can choose other objects of focus as well, such as an object that tends to have a calming or relaxing effect on you.

4. Focus

Once you have chosen an object of attention, get into a comfortable position and start focusing. Allow attention to be fully immersed and absorbed in the object, then let yourself relax and heighten awareness of the present moment. Resist the urge to let your mind drift elsewhere. Stay on the object.

5. Close gently

As you end the meditation, draw your attention back to your own body and feel yourself fully present in it. Imagine radiating peace all over you, from your eyes to your heart (Diksha, 2018).

6. Learn more

While these steps can give you an overview of what meditation should look like or what you can do to be in one, you may also want to go further by looking into books, websites, or web pages that focus solely on this matter. Here are a few suggestions:

Websites:

- https://thubtenchodron.org/

- https://insighttimer.com/sharonlaflamme/guided-med
  itations/serenity-meditation-for-people-who-are-stru
  ggling

- https://www.tenpercent.com/freeguidedmeditations

Books:

- *Serenity: Meditations of Acceptance, Courage* by Mikee
  Shea

- *Everyday Serenity* by Steven Kundtz David

- *Shortcut To Serenity: A Practical Guide to Developing a
  Peaceful Mind Through Meditation* by Nirav Shah

Chapter 5

Breaking Up With Isolation

"People are lonely because they build walls instead of bridges."
(Kingslover, 1988, p.232)

W e talked about how we can be quite chill about being by ourselves. That's a pretty important skill. After all, it is inevitable to almost always be in good company. Nevertheless, while everyone may benefit from some occasional alone time, it's still important to have connections and establish meaningful relationships with the people around us. Although there's no need to force yourself to be with others when you don't want to, you can build personal skills that might just come in quite handy every time you find yourself craving any sort of company. Here are a few tips:

Develop the courage to be disliked.

You read that right—the first step to feeling more at ease approaching people is realizing that some people are bound to dislike you in one way or another, and that's okay. You have to realize and remind yourself beforehand that people's reactions, including their perceptions and opinions of you, have nothing to do with your worth as a human being. More often than not, it has something to do with their own experiences, preferences, personal biases, and nothing to do with the fact that any of your personal characteristics are a good match or aren't. Attempting to control these things isn't only futile; it is also unnecessary. Quite frequently, those who are bound to like you will do so without you having to exert any effort to convince them, and those who are bound to dislike you will still do so no matter how much convincing you try to do. When you get used to the idea that people will always be divided in their perception of you, and that it's impossible to expect the whole world to love and care about you as much as you hoped, you get to free yourself from unrealistic expectations, and rest on the fact that, somehow, somewhere, there will always be people who'll appreciate you entirely as you are, see your imperfections, and love you anyway.

Be yourself.
Being yourself will lead you to people who share your interests. The less you become concerned about what people think of you, the more you will gain the courage to be yourself. Aside from this, being yourself is the first step in

finding the kind of people who will not only accept you for who you are but actually enjoy being with you. Of course, there are places where managing your impression of others and regulating your self-expression is necessary—such as in a corporate meeting—but these should be confined to situations where you don't necessarily expect to establish a long personal and emotional connection with the people involved. The rest of the time, muster the courage to just let yourself go—be authentically, unapologetically, and spontaneously you. Heads up, though—doing so might just turn some people off—the good news is, they're likely not the best people to surround yourself with—and those who stay and get to accept and appreciate you as you truly are usually worth keeping in life.

Start by talking to people with the same interests.
Relationships are built on conversations, and the easiest way to get a good one going is to discuss something you're passionate about with somebody who feels roughly the same way about it. So, don't be afraid to approach people who share your interest. Chances are, they'd be quite happy to connect. If you can't find anybody in your usual circle, allow yourself to venture out—reignite your passion for old hobbies, join special interest groups, or sign up for a preferred class. The bottom line? Meet new people, and don't limit your options.

If you're not used to approaching strangers, it may feel somewhat awkward at first. This is perfectly okay. Resist the urge to turn and run and just get on with it. If in doubt, don't hesitate to let the person do the talking. Resist trying to think of the right thing to say! There are no right words—just the right attitudes. Try to get yourself curious, for instance, about what the person is telling you at the moment, and the rest will follow. Admit to the person that you're nervous if you are, and try to find humor in the situation.

You may also want to take this side tip: keep in mind that the same interest doesn't necessarily mean the same thing, and it usually annoys the crap out of people when we tattle about how similar we are to them right off the bat, so be sure to avoid this. On top of it, be genuine—but don't sweat it out. Don't look at it like it's some mission or something. Just let the conversation flow and follow where it leads. In the end, it doesn't matter if you and the person you've just met might even end up as close friends; just try to enjoy the moment as it occurs. After all, if you keep doing this, you are bound to meet more people, and who knows? One or more of them is bound to be a nice new hobby buddy. For perspective, consider this quote by Fritz Pers:

"I do my thing, and you do your thing. I am not in this world to live up to your expectations, and you are not in this world to live up to mine. You are you, and I am I, and if by chance we find each other, it's beautiful. If not, it can't be helped; let it be" (Perls, 1969, p.4).

Don't close your doors to those who aren't like you.

The more you talk to people, the easier this thing becomes. As you feel yourself gaining more confidence, you may want to start to go beyond your usual common-interest groups. Go ahead. Try to do something new and allow yourself to keep meeting people, including those who seem the opposite of you. Think of it as planting seeds where, though not all would blossom into the rich, rewarding interpersonal connections we all crave, some of them just might—and that is a chance worth taking.

Try catching up with good old friends.

Of course, who would forget those we've known for years? We all have those bunch of really great friends we had when we were younger but, for some reason or another, somewhat drifted away from. If you feel like it, call one or a couple of them and arrange a date to catch up. Sometimes, nothing beats the company of good old friends.

Break up with isolation by building interpersonal connections.

The only way to befriend isolation is to break up with it. When we choose to upgrade our ability to form connections and be with other people, every bit of alone time becomes even more rewarding.

Chapter 6

Chasing Away the Blues

"I have depression. But I prefer to say, 'I battle' depression instead of 'I suffer' with it. Because depression hits, but I hit back. Battle on." (Kingslover, 1988, p.232)

D epression is no joke. Being the sneaky menace that it is; it can dump itself on the doorstep of the most unsuspecting people—even the most optimistic, well-loved bunch. It's not something we can easily get in and out of, that's for sure, and explaining it to others who have no inkling about what it's really like can be frustrating, exhausting, and downright heartbreaking. It's not something we could cure with a fine holiday quote, either.

Fortunately, its symptoms are identifiable, and with the right knowledge, intervention, and support, we are not entirely powerless. Depression is not a life sentence. Its presence in your life today doesn't have to cloud your future. You are not powerless, either. And despite what it may blatantly suggest, you are under no obligation to succumb to its whims.

Battling depression is never the easier route, but while the choice presents itself, grab hold of it. Depression takes so much from us; if we don't fight it, it will keep taking. It doesn't deserve free reign, and you deserve every bit of life you get back.

Taking the Enemy Apart

While we cannot control the weather outside of us, we can acquire the skills necessary to manage the one within us. Nevertheless, attempting to take on the enemy all at once can seem overwhelming, difficult, or even downright impossible. This said, one way to approach depression is to deal with its symptoms separately, from learning about them to identifying strategies, making sense of why these are likely to work, and eventually applying them.

<hr>

Strategies to Combat Common Depressive Symptoms

In the last chapter, we briefly talked about the common symptoms of depressive disorders. In this chapter, let us specifically look at the self-limiting symptoms of major depressive disorder (MDD), how they are usually experienced, and some helpful tips to deal with each.

Sleep Disturbance

Depression is frequently associated with poor sleep (National Library of Medicine, 2008). Some would describe not being able to sleep well, if at all, for weeks and months; others talk about sleeping excessively. And indeed, Nutt (2008) pointed out two types of disturbance: (1) insomnia (having trouble sleeping) and (2) hypersomnia (sleeping more often than normal). About 60% of young depressed adults experience insomnia, while about 40% experience hypersomnia, Nutt (2008) maintained.

Persons experiencing insomnia frequently report overthinking or excessive rumination as usual causes. More often than not, these individuals are caught in a vicious cycle: negative thoughts and emotions that usually accompany depression tend to get in the way of sleep, and a lack of sleep as well as poor quality sleep negatively impacts mood. Meanwhile, if we were to take a closer look at the anatomy and physiology behind our sleep-wake patterns, it may help shed light on the struggle. According to the National Institute of Neurological Disorders (n.d.), different parts of the brain work together to bring about and manage sleep functions. One receives information about light exposure; another keeps track of transitions between sleeping and waking up; and still, another produces the hormone melatonin, which helps us feel sleepy as soon as the lights grow dim.

Then there are these two internal biological systems—the circadian rhythm and homeostasis—that determine when you are awake and asleep. The former tunes your body clock with other environmental factors that affect sleep, while the latter keeps track of how much sleep you need as well as how much you are getting. Genes and neurotransmitters—those electrical messengers that carry information from nerve cell to nerve cell—also play a pivotal role in sleep. Some of these neurotransmitters signal the body to relax, while others, especially those designed to detect and alert the body of threats, make sure the body remains active and ready for movement, preventing relaxation. In short, there are a few things that promote sleep: low light, predictability, and relaxation. Conversely, there are a few things that prevent sleep: bright light, unpredictability, and alertness, often brought on by real or perceived threats. Drawing from these processes, here are a few tips:

Stay away from bright lights.
Blue light appears to be the worst of the most commonly used lights and—you guessed it—If you want to increase your chances of getting better sleep, stay away from your phone or laptop for at least thirty minutes to an hour before bed.

Be in bed at the same time every day.

You might argue that there's no use staying in bed when you know you won't be able to go to sleep anyway, and you might be right. However, going to bed at the same time every day—and staying away from this area the rest of the time as much as possible—will help the brain reassociate the bed with sleep. Don't think about having to go to sleep when you are in your bed, though, as this can backfire and make sleep even harder; instead, let yourself focus on the moment—on your breathing, the feel of your fingertips on the sheets, your toes on the bed board—every little thing around you. Try breathing consciously.

Quiet your thoughts.
Ask your thoughts to pause—yes, ask that part of you that keeps bringing negative stuff to your attention. Remind yourself where you are—in your bed and at home, for instance—so pausing would do no harm. Then, set aside time to worry about the next day, whether it's for five minutes, a quarter of an hour, half an hour, or an hour. What's important is that you leave space for the part of you that likes to think, so that when it's your turn to ask for a pause, you can do so confidently and with the hope that whatever worrisome event or possibility you are anticipating can be dealt with the next morning.

Focus on relaxation, not sleep.

If you have trouble sleeping, don't sleep. Just be with yourself and let yourself enjoy the stillness of the night. You see, if you turn your full attention to the hard goal—getting some sleep—you will miss out on the tiny, attainable goals that, when given attention, can lead you toward the bigger, seemingly impossible ones. So, now that we know that relaxation is one of the conditions that promote sleep, go for that one instead. In the event that sleep does indeed not come, laying down relaxed and aware of the present moment is the next best thing.

Anhedonia: Chronic Lack of Interest

The word anhedonia loosely translates to the inability to feel joy (Guo, 2023). This is often reflected in a notable lack of interest in activities one used to enjoy. This is a hallmark symptom of depressive disorders, but it can also occur among those who do not have any known health or mental health conditions, those with existing medical conditions, and those battling certain mental health disorders. Those who've been through it often describe how, to their bewilderment, joy becomes even more elusive than it ordinarily is. It is at that point in your experience where what used to be effective ways to make yourself happier suddenly stop working, and anything new that you try doesn't seem to generate enough joy either.

If you've battled with depression for some time now, you probably know how it feels like the back of your hand. You couldn't care less about things that used to catch your attention. Your passions appear to have lost their brilliance. Nothing matters anymore, or what used to mean so much to you just seems flat and unappealing all of a sudden. This is particularly noticeable to those around you, especially when you are known to be passionate about something and you flat-out refuse to get involved in anything related to it this time. A lot of those who experience it also describe a feeling of being stuck. Some would go on as far as to say that they'd rather be in the midst of an emotional rollercoaster than spend more time feeling stuck in what they'd describe either as a dark, dull vacuum or an unlit tunnel that stretches for miles and miles with no end in sight.

So, what do we know currently about this hallmark symptom? According to Gui (n.d.), anhedonia is most likely caused by "a decrease in activation of the region of the brain involved in reward and motivation," as well as a dysregulation of hormones and neurotransmitters responsible for regulating emotion and mood. Brodi (2022) differentiated between social and physical anhedonia. Social anhedonia, as Brodi (2022) explained it, is when you no longer feel up to meeting with others, even when there was a time when you did in the past. Physical anhedonia, on the other hand, is when you develop a repulsion for physical sensations, and things that used to bring you comfort, like long, tight hugs, can become overwhelming.

Meanwhile, since anhedonia can also come from medical conditions, such as thyroid problems, it is important to consult your professional healthcare provider to rule these out if you haven't already. Although there isn't currently any specific known cure for anhedonia, there are things you can do to help you navigate the experience more effectively and cope better. Here are some tips:

Do not identify with it.

Since most of us tend to identify with the things that make us happy, losing the ability to find joy in activities that used to give us pleasure can impact our sense of personal identity. Ultimately, we can begin to feel that our self as we know it is also slipping, and this realization can be even more painful than the thought of the possibility of never being able to find joy. When we begin to question our own identity, questioning our life's purpose and direction isn't too far off. So, if you can, differentiate yourself from the experience. Keep reminding yourself that, despite how it feels, you are still you to the very core. Everything you loved about yourself—you didn't lose it. You may have broken access to these for the time being, but deep inside you, no matter how much you seem to have changed, they are still there, waiting to welcome you back when you heal. Think of yourself as the sky, and all this—your depression, your anhedonia—are mere thunderclouds.

Clouds can block our view, obscuring both the sun and sky from our sight, but that doesn't mean they aren't there. Again, you are still you—don't let these experiences tell you otherwise. When a tree is cut down to a stump and regrows its vines in a different way or reaches for the sun in a different direction, it may look different, but it does not cease from being a tree. You carry every part of who you were as well as every part of who you are going to be. You've changed, and you'll keep on changing, experiencing both gains and losses throughout the process, but you are also the same person, and you'll get through this. So, keep hanging in there.

Realize that this does not make you any less strong.
Remember that, more often than not, anhedonia is physiological as well as psychological—it does not make one any less strong than they truly are, and it is definitely not your fault that you are experiencing this. You are not defined by your ability—or inability—to be happy, and joy is not the only thing that makes life meaningful. The more we understand this and release ourselves from the pressure of needing to feel good all the time, the more we are able to make room for enough peace so that maybe, just maybe, happiness will soon find us again.

Do not let joy be your reason for living.
More often than not, our source of joy is also where we derive our sense of purpose and direction—whether or not we are aware of it, we unwittingly make it our compass. Hence, the popularity of the phrase "follow our heart." Of course, we'd all agree that happiness is a highly sought-after ingredient for a

good life; nevertheless, we must not forget the fact that while joy enriches our experience and is indeed quite valuable, it does not contain the entirety of what it means to live a full life.

Understand that positive thinking won't always be able to rouse your spirits and it's okay.

People typically feel good upon reminding themselves of the good stuff. With anhedonia, however, the fact that no amount of good and nice can capture joy is a usual occurrence. This is why phrases that tend to work on inspiring others who aren't depressed, like "notice the good things" and "count your many blessings," don't work at all among people who experience anhedonia—if anything, they can leave you feeling worse. Sadly, few people understand this and, though quite well-meaning, more often than not, end up hurting us. There is something we can do, however, to lessen the blow, and that is to expect others to misunderstand. You see, all other people can see when they try to make sense of your situation is what is visible on the surface. A lot of the struggles we contend with aren't always written all over our faces. People have no obligation to dig deeper or to ask; all they can really do is take the information available to them and draw conclusions from it—conclusions that are, in a sense, quite limited and therefore least likely to be accurate. They are bound to misunderstand, and their reactions have nothing to do with our worth as individuals.

Aim for the habit, not the motivation.

Motivation fluctuates, but habits persist. Interest is good, but strategy takes us further. Unfortunately, we don't always realize this. So much emphasis has been placed on passion that, whether or not we are aware of it, it is easy to believe success isn't quite possible without it. One of the reasons why anhedonia can be so crippling is because we are used to the notion that the only way to achieve in life is to be extremely driven and enthusiastic about whatever it is that we want to excel at. As a result, we may opt to wait for motivation to strike before getting started and, more often than not, only perform our best when we are in high spirits. But then, it doesn't take a genius to see that, when you are dealing with anhedonia, this is definitely a bad idea. In this case, the motivation may not come.

So, what are we going to do then? The answer is, in fact, fairly simple: we turn to the next best thing—our ability to form habits. The advantage of habits is that they are almost, if not totally, automatic. That means these behaviors take less energy and effort on our part, and when we are battling with depression, we need all the extra energy we can get. But how do we acquire habits that are tailored to whatever it is we want to achieve? In his best-selling book, *Atomic Habits* (2018), James suggested that we break bigger habits into smaller ones that will eventually lead to the fulfillment of more complex goals. He discussed how, when we set our eyes on the smaller bits of the process, we become less overwhelmed. He also noted that what stops us from continuing towards the big goal when we reach a period of barely seeing progress is discouragement. That is, the more overwhelmed we are, the less confident we are about our ability to accomplish, and, consequently, the more discouraged we become. When we set goals that are so simple it is almost impossible to fail at them, however, success becomes a tiny but powerful motivator, and we become more likely to continue hitting one tiny fragment of the goal at a time consistently so that, as they accumulate, we also achieve more. Small progress is still progress, as Clear emphasized. In short, you don't have to be motivated or interested in something to be able to get it done. So, whenever you feel motivated, tell yourself to move a muscle—just one muscle—to obtain just one tiny prick of progress, because all progress, no matter how small, can lead us to the next one.

Depressed Mood

Depressed mood is another hallmark symptom of depressive disorders, particularly major depressive disorder. Some describe it as being in the water's depths or barely keeping yourself afloat in the middle of everything. Others describe it as a cruel blend of anhedonia and fatigue. Then, there were those who'd describe it as a subtle but persistent dread of yet another day. A depressed mood can present itself in many ways. For toddlers and young children, for instance, it often comes in the form of irritability and constant anger. Quite frequently, depression isn't about dark clothes and makeup, a gloomy face, or constant crying, as common sense would have us expect. It can be that eternally tightening knot in one's gut, all carefully tucked in with that easy-going smile one is able to master for months, weeks, maybe even years. It can be a longing for something one can't quite put their finger on. It sounds simple, but it can be crippling. While a depressed mood stemming from health or mental health issues doesn't usually go away despite our best efforts, much less disappear on its own, there is something we can do on our end to prevent it from wreaking further havoc with our lives or, at least to a certain degree, just give ourselves a bit of a leg up. Here are a few things you might want to try:

Stop trying to lift your mood.
It may sound counterintuitive, but trying to lift your mood in the midst of a depressed state is only going to make it more difficult. As mentioned earlier, having a condition like major depressive disorder means you won't be able to change your mood at will—at least not right away. Attempting to force it is not only futile—it also depletes your cognitive resources and strikes a massive blow on your self-efficacy (that sense of effectiveness or efficiency we all have), which of course gives self-concept and self-esteem that not-so-subtle nudge so they triple down like hopeless dominoes. Which, of course, leads to—you guessed it—a possibly worse mood afterward.

Therefore, while being depressed is no fun, rest in the comfort that you are not obliged to feel better—no matter what other people say—at the snap of a finger or upon hearing that mushy pep talk.

It's not that other people are out to make you uncomfortable. It's just that the rest of the world can have the best intentions and still end up hurting a depressed soul, so do focus your remaining strength on differentiating your situation from the way other people perceive it and trust your experience—every bit of it belongs to you, and no one can possibly know what it's like no matter how good you are at explaining—so let them not understand. Let them miss the point. And don't force yourself to fit into these molds. Don't force yourself to get out of a depressed mood like it's a mountain to conquer. In fact, stop thinking about moving mountains altogether. Think about how water brings incredible rock formations to life just by being water. How the ocean's gentle washing can smooth even the roughest rocks; how riverbeds are shaped by a steady flow as much as a raging current would. If you've come this far in the book, chances are you are already doing what you can—and that counts. Your task is not to battle a depressed mood—your task is to stand your ground until it passes and remind yourself it's okay to hold your breath for a second more.

Surround yourself with the right people (or stay away from the wrong ones).

Once in a while, we find people we can be safe with—you know those people—the kind that won't tell you how to think or what to feel; those that wouldn't demand an explanation over why you couldn't put on a smile that day or why you kept thinking about suicide the night before; those that are willing to sit with you whether you feel like venting or just keep your mouth shut. Surround yourself with these people. You don't have to tell them what you are going through. Just sit with them and get comfortable, and if possible, allow yourself to laugh with them.

Similarly, you'd want to minimize exposure to people who leave your mood in a worse state every time they come around. For instance, Drake (2021) of Psych Central warns about people who leave you "feeling confused and unsure of yourself; feeling drained, angry, or full of anxiety right after interacting with them; feeling bad about yourself in some way; or continually feeling the need to help them." These are often people who neglect to respect your boundaries or make you feel like you are walking on eggshells around them (Drake, 2021). These can be people who care a lot about you and whom you care a lot about in return. Should you cut ties with them then? The answer to that question can be quite complex, but generally, not exactly, or at least not in all cases—unless you throw violence or any form of aggression into the mix, of course. Take heed, however, about spending a good deal of your day around them. Or, if you can't help it, try to differentiate yourself from their suggestions and opinions as much as you can. You see, in this journey, you'd want to clear yourself of as much weight as you can while you heal. You'd want to be around those who contribute to your well-being and minimize exposure to those who don't.

Look for the tiniest thing that can shift your senses, and increase awareness of them.

Allocate a small part of your day for exploring and discovering things that have a positive effect on you—no matter how small. Let yourself experiment with things you like—or used to like, if you're in the middle of anhedonia—and be mindful of how these shift your senses. And don't forget the phrase "the tiniest shift." You see, in times where huge improvements take time and a lot more, it helps to celebrate the tiniest progress because they do eventually pile up, and what may seem insignificant at the moment can make a whole lot of difference sooner or later if you just keep at it. Noticing these little things helps us keep at it. To get started, here's a guide you may find quite helpful.

Step 1: Engage the senses.

Sight. According to Leder and his colleagues (2004), being in contact with things we consider beautiful can bring about positive emotions. "Aesthetic experience is emotionally positive and rewarding," Heshmat (2022) echoes in agreement. In other words, it matters what we see before us—literally. Recall that pleasant emotions tend to establish a good foundation for a positive mood. Logically, then, any opportunity to generate pleasant emotion is an opportunity to encourage a better mood as well. Consequently, notice how things in our visual field affect you, and then identify those that affect you positively and negatively. This way, you will be able to deliberately expose yourself to things that help and lessen, if not eliminate, those that don't. Here's a hint you may use as a guide:

Three things catch our attention when we engage our sense of sight. Start with these: color, lighting, and movement. For color, you may ask yourself, "How does blue—or any specific color, preferably what is dominant in your immediate environment—make me feel?" Get curious. What colors calm or excite you? What makes you feel just a teeny-weeny bit gloomier? For movement, try to recall if you typically prefer brightly lit or sun-flooded rooms, or pull down the drapes. Do you like yellow light—and if yes, do you prefer it dimly glowing in corners or boldly covering the whole space? For movement, let your eyes settle on things that gently move and also let them rest on still objects. Does calm, steady movement relax you? Tree branches swaying in warm, lazy afternoons; water and sea foam ebbing gently at the shore. Cat stretching across the lawn... Or do calm, airy interiors do the trick? If it's the latter, you may enjoy aesthetic videos of your choice.

Sound. It's no secret that music is an awesome mood-setter. It's been used for centuries to grace events, perform rituals, and even prepare troops for battle during the ancient wars.

According to an article posted in the Hindustan Times, for instance, "listening to sounds such as music and noise can have a significant impact on mood." It's no surprise that when we hear the word sound, we think of music almost immediately. According to Peltola and his colleagues (2016), "Even sad music brings listeners comfort."

Touch. Your fingertips can be a powerful tool for mindfulness. Experiment with letting it run through different textures, from smooth to rough to rugged, and describe the sensations in your head. Multi-textured objects like different types of fabrics are usually the go-to for most, but there's really no hard and fast rule.

Step 2: Notice the shift.

Whatever it is you pick, allow yourself to soak it in. Thereafter, notice if there is a shift in you. Notice if it felt good or uncomfortable, or if there was no shift. This is usually easier if you focus on the physical changes—a tightening or tingling sensation, perhaps, that either feels pleasant or unpleasant. Try out one, then move on to the next and the next, until you find those that do affect you positively.

Step 3: Acknowledge the shift and celebrate it.

Let even the smallest shift remind you that you are not stagnant. Increasing mindfulness over the little things allows us a whole new breadth of experience and reminds us that we don't always see everything there is. Not sensing hope, for instance, does not mean it isn't there.

⊰◦⊱

Follow that cliche advice: sunlight, nature, water, air, and gentle movements.

Environmental factors—not just your thoughts—have a significant impact on mood. So, if you can, try to manipulate your environment—or ask someone else to do so—in such a way that it promotes a mood-boosting effect. Generally, more sunlight is better, so open up those windows to let natural light in. Lightly colored walls are also preferred as opposed to darkly stained ones, so, if possible, have yours repainted to a lighter tone. If not, light-colored wallpapers can also be an option, as can painting only one side of the walls instead of all. You may also want to get close to the water—moving water especially: fountains, rivers, and seas. Decors that feature relaxing motions, such as those miniature tabletop fountains, can also be a nice addition to your space. These are just a few of the things you may want to try out.

Check your work-life balance; identify stuff you can let go of, and do it.

According to Sanfilippo (2023), "Balancing your professional and personal lives can be challenging, but it's essential." Denise Chilton (n.d.) listed eight signs of unhealthy work-life balance: never running out of things to do, consistently not getting enough sleep, intolerance to making mistakes, inability to spend time with significant people, constantly feeling irritable or on edge, a lack of self-care, trouble focusing, and an inability to recall the last time one actually had any fun. Experiencing any of these signals the need to cut yourself some slack. Work-life balance is essential for well-being, but it can be quite hard (Sanfilippo, 2023). HealthDirect suggests improving time management, setting limits, and prioritizing your health, among other things. If this doesn't put you back on track, identifying stuff you can let go of or pausing for a bit might help. The goal is to allow yourself some space to breathe while you are healing.

Outsource decluttering.

Everybody talks about decluttering their space, but nobody really talks about how hard it is when you are experiencing the blues. For starters, just assign one area you would like to declutter on your own, like your personal desk, and outsource the rest of it if you can. As Deng (2020) would put it, "There is no shame in asking for help." Clutter contributes negatively to mental health. And of course, quite obviously, keeping your personal living space—be it at work or in the house—as clean and clutter-free as possible goes a long way.

Concentration Problems

Once in a while, we may experience difficulty concentrating—whenever we are preoccupied with thoughts of something else, for instance, or when the environment distracts us from focusing. In depression, though, we can have trouble concentrating even without interference. A lot of those who struggled with similar problems would say that it feels like fragments of your thoughts are slipping away: like it is difficult to grab hold of one and connect to the others somewhat. Some would describe it as being mentally slow or liken it to a slow-loading computer program. Some also point out increased forgetfulness or memory loss (Theobald, 2013).

According to research, depression impairs the capacity to rapidly and efficiently incorporate information (Theobald,

2013). You may have difficulty giving directions as well as understanding them, which in turn can impact how one conducts themselves in areas of their lives requiring them to function or accomplish certain tasks—like at work or in school. To overcome this, Theobald (2013) suggested three things that can help, aside from undergoing treatment, which he also suggested. These are as follows: remediation techniques, compensatory strategies, and adaptive approaches. In case you wanted to try it out for yourself, here are a few examples:

Remediation Techniques
1. Computer Programs or Applications
There are a lot of computer programs and applications designed to help people concentrate. For instance, here are eight suggested *focus* apps according to Zapier.com:

- **Freedom:** for blocking distractions on all your devices at once

- **Cold Turkey Blocker:** for scheduled system-wide blocking

- **LeechBlock NG:** for free browser-based website blocking

- **RescueTime:** for time tracking with built-in website blocking

- **Forest:** for motivating you to put your phone down

- **SelfControl:** for a nuclear option

- **PawBlock:** for distraction blocking with cute animal picture

- **Focus:** for a combination Pomodoro timer and distraction blocker

2. **Written Exercises**

Journaling can help you explore your inner experiences in a safe, non-threatening manner. Practicing mindfulness by describing every minute detail of your physical environment, for instance, helps you learn to ground yourself in the here and now, even when you have no previous training or experience doing this. All you have to do is get your pen and notebook ready and just start scribbling away, covering the space you are currently in from corner to corner. You can start with where you connect with it (for example, describe your position and what part of you touches the environment), like this: "I am now sitting in a wooden chair, and I can feel the firm concrete floor beneath my feet. The floor is made of cold white tiles." Nonetheless, there's really no hard and fast rule. Just be your free, authentic self.

Compensatory Strategies

Compensatory strategies involve the conscious effort to manage the lack of a certain skill by maximizing the use of another. It rests on the premise that since there are many ways to accomplish things, losing one skill doesn't necessarily have to leave us handicapped; other skills can be used in its place. If you haven't done this already, begin by checking out the skills you have at the moment as well as those that you may still need to work on improving when you're ready. Then, use what you're good at to make up for what you're not. Here's a step-by-step guide to walk you through the process:

Step 1: Here is a list of cognitive or thinking abilities. Circle the ones you do best and box the ones that you find difficult.

- **Pay attention:** the ability to direct your attention towards what you would like to attend to.

- **Remain focused:** retain attention despite the presence of environmental or internal interferences.

- **Remember:** be able to easily recall learned information or memory of an event.

- **Understand instructions:** easily grasp spoken or written procedures, requests, and directions.

- **Recognize the pattern of events:** to identify relationships between events; determine how fragments of information can go together; can make associations; and organize information easily so it is easily understood.

- **Analyze problems**: to identify pros and cons of existing concerns and make decisions based on available information.

- **Troubleshoot solutions:** to evaluate thought-up solutions to existing concerns or modify them according to newly acquired information in order to enhance effectivity.

Step 2: Look at the ones you have circled. These are your strengths. Reflect on them using these guide questions:

1. What came to your mind when you looked at the list?

2. How do you feel about each skill?

3. How does each skill help you make day-to-day routine activities less of a grind?

4. How does each skill help you deal with any of the MDD symptoms we mentioned earlier?

Step 3: Look at the ones you've boxed. These are either abilities hampered by your depression or areas you may still need to improve on. Reflect on them using these questions:

    1. What came to mind when you looked at the list?

    2. How do you feel about each skill?

    3. What were the common concentration-related difficulties you've had during the past two weeks?

    4. How does not being able to fully utilize these skills impact your adjustment in relevant areas (home, school, or work relationships and task performance, etc.)?

    5. What tools have you tried using in an attempt to supplement your current skill level?

Step 4: Think of usual scenarios where you might need some of these skills and recall your latest experience related to them.

Pay attention to how you coped and how the presence of one skill can compensate for the absence of another. Take note of the things you have learned.

Step 5: Come up with a strategy using the information you gathered about yourself and try it out. Then, evaluate the outcome.

If it helps, turn it into a habit. If it did, but only barely, make some adjustments and try it again. If it didn't, switch to another strategy. Also, don't forget to be kind to yourself through this. Remember, the concentration problem stemming from depression doesn't just go away, even if you've done everything right. Trying to help yourself is already a big leap, whether or not it turns out as smoothly as you'd hoped.

Adaptive Approaches
    1. Make changes in your environment.

Remove anything that distracts. If possible, avoid hoarding unnecessary objects or get rid of those you already have right away. Position things in easy-to-reach areas, and make sure your spaces are well-ventilated and neither too hot nor too cold. If a certain type of music helps you focus, turn it on. If not, keep your place nice and quiet. There are a lot of other things you can do. Allow yourself to get creative as you try things out. If all these aren't possible, work on changing your mindset about your immediate environment; don't be afraid to start with the littlest thing.

    2. Make use of available tools

Calendars, planners, alarm clocks, checklists: these are things we'd easily find on our phones. But in case that doesn't work for you, feel free to grab any of their tangible counterparts.

3. Tap your inner resources.

We all have a wealth of resources inside us, and you won't ordinarily stumble upon somebody who has it all, but the more you become consciously aware of what you have, the more you will be able to use it as well. It's okay to have difficulties; it's also okay to have seemed to lose some of their strength because of depression for the time being. Remember that healing cannot be rushed, but, as we've mentioned earlier, even the slightest progress can take you to greater heights, so give yourself some slack and allow yourself to breathe. It isn't easy; this only shows how strong you are.

◆◇◆

Excessive Guilt

Guilt is an exhausting feeling, particularly if it's been bugging you for some time. It's not something you can easily push out of your headspace either. Sometimes, it's like a solid knot that builds just below your chest—a tightness that can crawl steadily from the back of your spine to the tip of your ears, or all over—other times, like a cloak over your head. Guilt—regret and apprehension of wrongdoing—can be overwhelming. North Carolina Psychiatrist, Harold Hong (2022) describes it as "an emotional experience that occurs when a person believes or realizes—correctly or incorrectly—that they have compromised their values or morality in some way (Gillette, 2022)." Consequently, Gillette believed that a lot of our feelings of guilt come from either the desire to treat others well—especially those that matter to us—or from the fear of any sort of punishment or negative consequence, which, psychoanalyst Sigmund Freud argued, is shaped by the child's interaction with their primary caregiver—usually their parents.

Guilt can present itself in many ways. For instance, research by Basile and her colleagues (2010), focused on the most common two: one coming from the perception of going against your own values or morals (deontological guilt), and another brought about by empathetic feelings for someone who you think you wronged (empathetic guilt). Hoffman (2018), on the other hand, talked about a third type of guilt, not mentioned by Basil and the others: existential guilt—one that comes from not living out your own purpose for existing or not being able to maximize your innate potential.

But then, guilt doesn't always come from what we've done or failed to do. Yamagishi (2014), for one, discussed another type of guilt—one less talked about: non-related guilt, or "a guilt that arises without any clear relationship between one's actions and an outcome," as Gillette would say. This is just like the survivor's guilt, where one can feel guilty about not dying or suffering like the others, or feel unworthy of having been the one who made it among close family members or friends. In this case, the person did nothing against their morals or to deliberately harm others: the distress caused, however, can be just as strong as with the other forms, sometimes maybe stronger.

That said, Yamagishi's research should remind us that guilt doesn't always come from an undesired outcome of our actions. Of all types, the last one could be particularly concerning because it involves feeling guilty when it is not your fault: a clear form of self-sabotage. Unfortunately, this kind of guilt is common among individuals who battle depression—in which case it often comes in excessively. The good news is, there is a way to lessen the impact of excessive guilt on you. For starters, you've got to grab hold of the keys: awareness, tolerance, and strategy.

Awareness. Knowing that guilt can come in many forms is vital at identifying which kind of guilt is weighing you down at the moment. Afterall, it will be very difficult, if not impossible, to overcome something you know nothing of. You have to tell whether your guilt comes from the outcome of your actions or from unfounded assumptions, or automatic thoughts that come from irrational beliefs. This is important because how you approach and deal with the experience will differ based on these two. One way to do this, according to Gillette, is to keep this in mind: when you feel guilty over something you did, it's usually not that hard to point out why;

but with non-related guilt, it can feel like finding a needle in a haystack. Quite frequently, with the latter, one has to contend with emotions arising from thoughts like "I should have" or "shouldn't have," followed by something you couldn't have realistically done. For example: "I should have known the early signs of cancer," isn't realistic at all, but being guilty over this thought can just be as distressing as being guilty about deliberately lying or shoplifting.

It is particularly difficult when you start feeling guilty over things you have little to no control over. In a web article, Smith (2023) outlined ways to deal with excessive guilt. He talked about identifying the source, remaining open about your emotion, being willing to correct mistakes when needed and then finding ways to do so. He also talked about pausing to refocus on something else whenever it becomes too overwhelming and being kind to oneself and others. Further ahead, he believed in focusing on what you can do on your end, considering alternative ways of behaving the next time you encounter a similar situation, and changing self-talk into more adaptive ones.

Identifying the source of your feelings of guilt may not be as easy as it sounds. But with the right information and tools in your hand, this is attainable.

Start by defining your experience. You can use these questions as a guide:

1. What particular outcome do you deem yourself responsible for? (Write this down as specific as possible)

2. What specific behavior of yours contributed to the outcome?

3. What do you think about this behavior? Why is it acceptable or not acceptable?

4. What moral principles did you breach when you did or failed to do the preferred behavior?

5. How connected are your preferred behavior and the distressing outcome?

6. How would you feel if another person engaged in this behavior? Would you feel the same thing if it were you doing it instead? Why do you think this is so?

7. Do you think the behavior is like you or unlike you? Why or why not?

8. What should you have done? How possible was it, given the circumstances of that moment?

9. If a similar event would happen again, what circumstances will help you engage in your preferred behavior? Are these circumstances within your control? Why or why not?

10. Looking at your answers, which of the following describes the kind of guilt you experience best?

- Deontological guilt: I did something that isn't like me, or I did something that violates my philosophy in life or moral conviction.

- Empathetic guilt: I did something I don't approve of and it had a negative effect on those involved.

- Existential guilt: I am not living my life to the fullest; I am less than what I should have become at this point.

- Non-related guilt.

- I don't deserve to have it easier than the others.

- The outcome happened because I hoped, wished for, or imagined it.

- I don't deserve all the attention.

- I don't deserve the favors I am getting.

- I am weighing other people down.

- I am making things more difficult for other people.

If you're done with this exercise, don't forget to appreciate yourself! It isn't easy exploring difficult experiences like these, but you mustered the courage to do it! As you've probably noticed at this point, doing so allows you the opportunity to not just understand your situation, but also gain insight on what could possibly help you get yourself unstuck.

Tolerance. Awareness doesn't just come with new insights and motivators—whether we like it or not, it can come with pain or distress as well. This brings us to the next key: tolerance. Yes, to be able to get ourselves out of a storm, we first have to muster the courage to withstand it—and this can involve living with distressing emotions for quite a bit before finally being able to let them go. Every emotion demands to be felt, not just pain, as John Green (2012) said. Allowing yourself to feel the emotion, and holding your ground as the storm passes, lets you get out of its grip faster than denying or trying to resist it. So, if you are feeling just a little bit worse after your attempt to raise your awareness about this whole thing, you should know that this is a good sign. Now, let that thought sink in because this isn't a popular bit. Pain is a good sign. It means you have gotten yourself unstuck from the vacuum, and, as you raise tolerance of the distress, it begins to lose its power over you, and you begin to regain your power over it.

Strategy. The third key is strategy. As mentioned earlier, depending on the type of guilt you are experiencing at the moment, you may have to look into different strategies to cope. Let's take a look at each one and explore potential strategies that might help. Keep in mind though, that these are only a few of the many. If you go to therapy, for instance, your therapist might be able to help you discover more, or guide you into implementing these or some of which you might just develop on your own along the way.

How to Deal With Deontological Guilt
1. Verbalize the action believed to have caused the outcome (or write it down and then read it aloud.).

2. Explore your beliefs about the action causing the distress.

3. Figure out whether the action causing the distress is an unwanted habit or a one-time occurrence.

4. Figure out if it is a decision or an impulse.

5. Revisit the source of conviction for your beliefs.

6. Explore the personal or subjective significance of your convictions.

7. Identify ways to avoid unwanted behaviors in the future.

8. Recognize that your spiritual or philosophical journey is a moment-by-moment decision.

9. Manage your expectations for yourself.

10. Forgive yourself.

Perspective

Most of us wanted to do well—that is, to be a good person. Our idea of what good is, however, varies to a great extent. We tend to use a certain guide or a moral compass to determine which actions are acceptable and which aren't—it can be as loose as some random cultural mores and folkways you're constantly exposed to throughout life or as tangible and personal as a religious or motivational book you actually care about. Our values system—often derived from religious and cultural influences and the breadth of other psychosocial experiences we get immersed in—is also another thing that sits with us each time we attempt to gauge or evaluate our actions from a moral perspective. When we're satisfied with the evaluation, we tend to feel good about ourselves and motivated to do better; when we're not, we might feel sad, guilty, or even unworthy.

The more you explore your beliefs about the action causing the distress, the more your feelings about it will make sense. The more it makes sense, the less you'll feel powerless over the guilt present and the situation in general. That said, coming up with solutions can become your new priority—something that works best in the long run. For instance, to deal with incongruence, you can either choose to change or honor the belief. This would require you to either manage your present behavior so that the unwanted one doesn't get repeated (if you decide to stick to the belief that it's wrong) or assimilate new information to reforge a new perspective that, when applied, is more realistic or attainable (if you decide to modify or even ultimately ditch the belief that caused you to feel guilty in the first place). The former rests on the premise that while some people are quite comfortable changing compasses—ditching a personal philosophy that is no longer helpful, for instance, or even switching religions—others feel quite appalled by even the mere thought of that, especially if this precept is already a huge part of their identity—and that's okay. The latter, on the other hand, rests on the premise that, more often than we'd like to admit, sometimes we do adapt beliefs that encourage us to place unrealistic demands upon ourselves, putting us at risk of setting ourselves up for failure—that is, never measuring up. This can send us into a downward spiral of guilt and self-doubt—exactly what you're trying to overcome at this point.

How to Deal With Empathic Guilt

1. Verbalize the action that caused the outcome.

2. Explore the extent of your participation or contribution to the outcome objectively.

3. Verbalize the effect of the outcome on the people

involved.

4. Figure out if the action is habitual.

5. Plan out ways to replace an unwanted habit with an acceptable one.

6. Express your thoughts and feelings to the people involved.

7. Have the courage to risk trusting others.

8. Forgive yourself.

9. Consider apologizing.

10. Realize that every person is responsible for their own emotions; you are not obliged to treat other people well, and neither are they.

How to Deal With Existential Guilt
1. Imagine the life you want.

2. Break down the different elements of the life you want: what is it made of?

3. Restructure your idea of a good life: eliminate wants that are unrealistic or unattainable, and replace them with the next best thing.

4. Detach yourself from any sort of achievement timeline.

5. Identify the skills you wish to develop.

6. Research the available avenues for learning these skills.

7. Forget your age. Learn these skills.

8. Let go of other people's opinions.

9. Focus on the present.

10. Focus on what can be done.

11. Do it.

How to Deal With Non-Related Guilt
1. Stop identifying with your thoughts.

2. Never belittle yourself for believing in something, no matter how flawed.

3. Remind yourself that there is no right way to feel.

4. Become aware that there is a right way to think.

5. Admit that it is not possible to get all information, so always leave room for possibilities other than what is most likely.

6. Give yourself the benefit of the doubt.

7. Realize that your assumptions might just be wrong.

8. Imagine the worst and prepare for it.

9. Acknowledge the possibility of a better outcome.

10. Understand and accept that some things are not within your control.

11. Focus on what is within what you can do.

12. Learn specific strategies.

Cognitive Reframing: The Art and Science of Changing Your Mind

People don't like changing their minds. We are, as Sandle (2016) would put it, "generally stubborn." The fact that we tend to give less weight to evidence that goes against our views and more weight to evidence that supports them, (Wason, 1960) doesn't help either. Nevertheless, cognitive psychologists like Ellis (1962) and Beck (1963) believe that the ability to change our minds is a valuable therapeutic tool (Austad, 2009) and, while it can be challenging to take on, particularly at first, it is something most anyone could learn to do. We have a word for this, actually: cognitive reframing, and this can be done either with a therapist or on your own. The effectiveness of this technique has also been well established since its introduction (Marasigan, 2019), and continues to be used extensively by professionals in the mental health field.

In the height of emotional distress, it's easy to feel stuck in a loop of endless negatives. When done right, cognitive reframing can be like a breath of fresh air. Morin (2022) compares it to looking through a telescope or a camera lens, where zooming in and out can produce an entirely different experience, even when you're looking at the same thing. Sometimes, a new outlook is all you need to get yourself unstuck.

The Process

There are many ways to reframe your thoughts. One of which is Albert Ellis' ABCDE Technique, where one moves through a five-step process, each represented by a letter broadly hinting at what has to be done:

1. Activating agent

The activating agent is any event that is perceived to have caused the emotion. Take note of the word "perceived" because, in reality, events don't cause emotions—the belief about them does. However, people notice the events preceding the emotions more than they notice the beliefs or assumptions that come after them, so it's very common to associate how we feel with what has happened before that. That said, two people can go through the same circumstance and have very different emotional experiences.

2. Belief
The belief is what underlies your thoughts about the event. As soon as you've identified the event closest to the emotion you are working on, try to explore what you think about it. You can ask yourself questions like: "What's the first thing that came to mind right after it (the event) happened?"

3. Consequence
The physiological responses and emotions that follow. Once you've figured out the belief that came right after the event, recall the physiological responses and emotions that followed suit. Notice that if your belief about the event is negative, the resulting emotion can be unpleasant as well. Meanwhile, the less negative the belief, or the more it leaves room for something good, the less emotional distress you are likely to experience.

4. Disputation
Disputation is simply questioning the thoughts and beliefs that caused the distressing emotion. Here, you can check for

cognitive biases. You can also identify which of your beliefs are realistic and which aren't.

5. Effective new belief

The last part of Ellis' process is to decide which beliefs are best accepted, rejected, or modified. This is the point of the whole thing.

The Cognitive Biases

In her book, *Counseling and Psychotherapy Today*, Carol Austad (2009), outlines different irrational processes (according to Ellis) and cognitive biases (according to Beck) that get in the way of clear thinking. We will list ten of them here, with a brief description on the side. Feel free to check them out, and when you're up to it, try to examine yourself based on the guide question that follows.

- Demandingness: the belief that unless a set of rigid "oughts", "shoulds", and "musts" are met, life is not worth living and one can never be really happy.

Example: A person might rigidly believe that unless they are accepted in their first interview, their whole career is in jeopardy; unless they get married at a specific age, they wouldn't be able to obtain the joy and stability they deserve; or unless they never yell at their toddler, they're a bad parent.

- Awfulizing: the belief that the worst is always bound to happen.

Example: A student who fails a short quiz might come to the conclusion that they will fail the whole course altogether; a person who is having recurrent migraines might begin to stress that they have cancer; a teacher who unwittingly cut a student with an unkind remark is convinced they've scarred them for life.

- Low frustration tolerance: being totally convinced that difficult things are unbearable.

Example: A person may be rigidly convinced that they cannot live without their ex; that failing at something they highly value would cost them their sanity; or that their current feelings of guilt or remorse about forgetting their sick mom's birthday are unbearable.

- Arbitrary inference: stubbornly sticking to an interpretation formed based on some random choice or assumption rather than on a logical explanation or the presence of enough evidence. This may also involve rejecting evidence that runs contrary to your interpretation.

Example: Being convinced that nobody cares for them despite family members and friends consistently coming over and showing signs of genuine caring or concern; or an accident is your fault because you dreamt about it before it happened.

- Dichotomous thinking: seeing anything or anyone as entirely of one characteristic or the other, such as good or only bad, right or wrong, and refusing to acknowledge anything can exist in between.

Example: A friend is a really bad mom for spanking their toddler occasionally; a neighbor is a horrible person for not coming in to say hello on your first day; or the new boss is immoral for not sharing your own religious or political views.

- Magnification and minimization: exaggerating problems, even when they're obviously petty, or denying the gravity of the situation, even with various evidence pointing to a serious situation.

Example: Laughing off a supervisor's warning when they are clearly about to lose their job or being convinced that they are eventually getting fired for incurring three absences in a row after getting sick.

- Personalization: blaming oneself for an event or situation despite lacking evidence. This can also mean thinking that every single negative event has its roots in one's own unworthiness, bad luck, or wrongdoing.

Example: Blaming oneself for a friend's misfortune because they're angry at them.

- Over-generalization: applying a concept inferred from an isolated incident as a general rule to evaluate other unrelated events

Example: Adopting the belief that all men (or women) are cheaters after having been cheated on a couple of times.

- Selective abstraction: interpreting information incorrectly and refusing to change, similar to David Burn's negative mental filter.

Example: Being utterly convinced that learning a song on a recorder is impossible because they suck at piano lessons.

Excessive guilt often stems from thoughts like these. They are considered biased and quite unhelpful, if not downright self-defeating. By over focusing on some (usually negative) and ignoring other (usually positive) information, they don't only elicit emotional distress, they also keep you from seeing the real score, coming up with a viable solution, coping, or ultimately solving the problem at hand.

Now that you know what cognitive biases are, it's time to check out your thoughts and reflect on whether or not you harbor some of them. Based on Ellis' Rational Emotive Therapy, here are steps you can take, followed by some tips on how to dispute or challenge these thoughts and replace them with more realistic or logical ones (Austad, 2009).

Tips for Identifying Beliefs
1. Be honest.

2. Be objective.

3. Momentarily put feelings aside.

4. Suspend judgment.

Tips for Disputing Irrational Beliefs
1. Ask questions.

2. Consider logic.

3. Consider available evidence supporting the belief.

4. Consider probability.

5. Identify what keeps you clinging to the belief.

6. Imagine the worst.

7. Be willing to change irrational beliefs.

Characteristics of Effective New Beliefs

1. They leave room for modification.

2. They consider all possibilities.

3. They are not superlative.

4. They differentiate the belief from the person who believes them.

5. They are realistic.

6. They do not include unrealistic demands.

7. They can be replaced to accommodate new information or new learning.

Psychomotor Retardation and Energy Loss

It's not uncommon to feel downright lethargic when the blues hit. According to the American Psychological Association (2015), psychomotor retardation and energy loss often accompany bouts of depressive episodes. Purse (2023) describes it as "moving, speaking, reacting, and often thinking more slowly than normal." Now, that may sound like something that could happen to anyone under a lot of stress but, this is nowhere near like coming down tired after extraneous physical activity or a long day at work. For one, it often doesn't go away or get better with rest. In fact, it is not uncommon for those who experience it to get hit at the very start of the day. It can present itself in a lot of ways: you may feel sluggishness when walking or changing positions, for instance, or have difficulty performing tasks that require eye-hand coordination and fine motor skills. You may notice slower reactions to situations or difficulty keeping up good posture.

People may tell you you've been responding more slowly or quietly than usual, or that your voice has taken on a monotonous tone. They may notice those long pauses you have to take in the middle of a sentence when you talk. You yourself may notice the frequent lost trains of thought. People may catch you staring into space and express their concerns (Purse, 2023). A lot of those who experience this describe it as a feeling of heaviness that is almost literal—like having a weighted jacket on. Even the simplest activities can feel like a stretch—a couple of meters walk to the shower can feel like miles, a trip to the nearest grocery store even worse. Unfortunately, this may easily pass off as being lazy or choosing to slack off and leave those who experience it feeling guilty or inefficient. When coping with psychomotor retardation and energy loss, Purse recommends giving yourself some grace. Be kind to yourself. Take time to adjust. Remind yourself that you are not just lazy and that this is part of a condition that, with the right intervention and support, does get better. On a practical note, break down big tasks into smaller ones, and outsource some of the things you have to do if you can. Avoid comparing yourself with others, and don't give up! It might be easier said than done, but it's not impossible.

<hr>

Thoughts of Dying or Killing Oneself

Suicidal ideation is more common than we think, not just among those diagnosed with depression. It isn't the same for everybody. Dealing with suicidal thoughts can be tough as well. If you are having suicidal thoughts, it is best to seek help as soon as you can. Meanwhile, here are a few things you might want to keep in mind:

1. *Thoughts of dying or killing yourself do not make you a bad person.* Thoughts are neither good nor bad, and they have nothing to do with who you are as a person.

2. *Thoughts are rough sketches, not blueprints.* Your thoughts aren't facts or predictions either—they are valuable sources of information about our current needs, but they are in no way predictive of what happens next.

3. *Thoughts of dying or killing yourself are often byproducts of exhaustion and hopelessness.* Death becomes appealing not because we no longer want anything to do with life, but because we don't want to keep living in the same situation that we are currently in.

4. *It's best to take it one day at a time.* Focusing on the future may trigger anxiety. Focusing on the past can cause bouts of regret. Shifting our attention to the present encourages problem-solving because it is the only point in time where we can actually do something on our end, no matter how small.

5. *Most people may not understand.* Suicide is a tough topic. The world is only beginning to become aware that talking about it helps link valuable resources to those who need them. A lot of people are still afraid to make the mistake of saying something that would push them to the edge. While most of the significant people in your life are genuinely concerned, expect that they won't be able to fully grasp the depth of

your experience. As a result, some may overreact while others may brush it off. It doesn't mean they care any less.

6. *Seeking help does help.* A lot of mental health and other wellness professionals are trained to help individuals through extremely difficult experiences. They can also teach you the skills necessary to get over rash and impulse-based decision-making, especially when it comes to major life choices.

To Sum It Up

The only way to chase away the blues is to take an active role in your own journey to heal. This can be lonely, exhausting, and isolating as a lot of people simply may not understand, even when they try to. Stand your ground. And don't forget, while it may seem like you're all alone right now, someone else is probably navigating the same seas only a few miles away. You are not entirely alone.

Chapter 7

Life Is an Adventure

"It is not the things we do in life that we regret on our deathbed. It is the things we do not."

Nourishing Your Venturesome Soul

If you look up the word adventure, you'll likely come across three things: dangerous, unpredictable, and exciting. That's exactly how life is. Whether we like it or not, there will always be threats around us, and as much as security and stability sound good, life will never cease to surprise us. Whether or not we find life exciting, however, is entirely up to us. And, more often than not, this boils down to our attitude because whenever we are presented with a choice—to allow ourselves to wait in eager anticipation of the next big challenge or to cower in our corners and hide away—it is the kind of attitude we have towards life and living that'll push us on one side or the other. So, take a moment to pause and ponder what you've been doing lately. Are you making the most of every moment or simply killing time? When loneliness or depression strikes, do you allow yourself to get curious about what might just be waiting around the bend or just let yourself sink passively underneath?

You see, as appealing as stability and consistency are, we are not made to spend the rest of our days killing time. We are made to flourish. Flourishing requires growth. But growth, no matter how subtle, is near impossible without change. Sometimes, change is painful, and since we don't usually like pain, we shy away from it altogether, throwing away any opportunity to grow with it. But as Stoic philosopher Augustus famously said, "If you want a rainbow, you would have to put up with the rain." Sometimes we have to let go of things that matter to us just to get to a place that matters more. We put up with losses more often than we'd like and just take that one big leap even when faith isn't our thing. A lot of times, winning won't look a lot like winning on the outside either. Meanwhile, adventures don't have to be grand. In fact, it can be quite simple and still count. Here are a few things, for instance:

Identify what holds you back.
Anything can hold us back—from feelings, fear, or apprehension to a number of practical things. Identifying what these are will help you come up with ways to deal with them.

Discover what you are afraid of.

Our fear can tell us a lot about ourselves, such as what matters to us. Afraid of getting hurt? Life matters to us. Afraid of hurting others? We care about significant people. Afraid of making mistakes? We want to do things right.

By being curious about what we are afraid of and exploring how this might be so, we don't only make it less threatening; we also give ourselves the opportunity to act on our fear objectively and sensibly. In doing so, we get to still do what we can to safeguard what matters to us and we don't end up doing so blindly and throwing away the opportunity to enjoy life in instances where doing so would have been unnecessary.

Start doing tiny, brave things.

As mentioned earlier, adventures don't have to be grand. Courage doesn't have to be big and bold. Sometimes, it is overcoming little things that make the most impact. So go ahead and set yourself up for the smallest successes. Start letting yourself do things you are nervous about, and commend yourself for being brave enough to do them.

Upgrade your current skills.

Go back to what you love doing and get better at it. The better we become at doing something, no matter how simple, the more it boosts our confidence and self-esteem, and the more this happens, the less likely we are to subconsciously push people away. So go on and remember all the things you could do well and build on them further. Refuse to be stagnant. Propel yourself towards growth and forget about the speed of the process. Take it nice and slow, relish every moment, and don't forget to celebrate small wins.

Learn new things.
Our skills can take us places, and this opens up more opportunities to meet others. Remember that every person you meet is a potential kindred soul, so keep grabbing any opportunity to do just that.

Make a bucket list.
Bucket lists never get old. So go ahead and think of all the things you want to do, list them down, and start making plans to get to them. You can rank them according to attainability but don't get yourself stuck on a timeline. Your bucket list has to be flexible, too. Keep in mind the unpredictability of life, but turn it to your advantage by always leaving room for changes in your plans and making every moment count.

Take that first step out of the door.
You can have all the other tips in place, but unless you lift your feet and carry yourself out the door, you won't really get anywhere, so let yourself go. Wear that string of wisdom nuggets you've collected all this time, and cloak yourself in courage and anticipation. Enjoy the sun on your skin and don't hide. So much of life awaits.

Finding Your Meaning and Purpose

According to Dr. Frankl, the creator of logotherapy, "Life is never unbearable by circumstances, but only by a lack of meaning and purpose" (Austad, 2009). In his book, *The Will to Meaning*, he talks about how suffering doesn't really come from adversity. In other words, no amount of circumstance could really rob us of our joy—unless it got to rob us of our sense of meaning and purpose first. These two, according to Frankl, are our primary motivators. They keep us going, even against all odds. Without these, we are fickle or easily swayed by whatever life throws at us. The Merriam-Webster's Dictionary associates the word meaning with the word significance—value, importance, a "quality worthy of attention"—something that matters. Simply put, we all wanted our lives to count, whether we'd admit it or not.

Meanwhile, it isn't always easy to find meaning in life. The topic has been subject to philosophical inquiry for centuries, that's for sure. So, if you feel like you don't know yours, rest in the fact that you aren't the only one. For most, finding meaning is a lifelong process. We don't just stumble upon our own meaning, Frankl believes. We don't create it either. We have to discover it, he says, and to do that, we've got to have the will to. According to Pattakos (2018), "meaning is different for everyone—there is no one right answer—there is only the answer that is right for you." Pattakos also talked about how our meaning is deeply connected to what he referred to as our core essence—our true selves. He further pointed out that this meaning doesn't have to be something huge; in fact, it could be found in a lot of little good things. The more we allow ourselves to honestly admit what truly matters to us, the closer we become to discovering our meaning, and with that comes the next big thing: purpose.

Purpose, as mentioned, is another propeller. It gives us a reason for being; it shapes our goals and guides what we do. A person who has a clear sense of purpose is less likely to get distracted by life's challenges. They are also less likely to give up. And just like your meaning, your sense of purpose is largely subjective. Nobody else can define it for you. Of course, the world can offer suggestions, but ultimately, you would have to be the person to take your pick.

Life is indeed an adventure, and like all adventures, it has so much in store for us. It has so much in store for you. And it may not seem like it right now, but the world does keep turning around. There is so much you have to discover for yourself, and the more you allow yourself to do just this, the more you get to stumble upon the hidden gems of you—and the best news is, each piece you stumble upon can only ignite that will to find more.

Chapter 8

Beating the Blues With a Bigger Perspective

"When one door closes, another door opens, but we so often look so long and so regretfully upon the closed door, that we do not see the ones which open for us." (Kingslover, 1988, p.232)

According to Heshmat (2017), "Adopting a self-distanced perspective can help us face negative thoughts and emotions without becoming overwhelmed by them" (Kross and Ayduk, 2008). This is especially helpful when we are battling with either a depressed mood or emotional turmoil. "A broader perspective allows us to consider multiple aspects of a situation," Heshmat went on. This isn't easy to attain when you're in the depths, but it isn't impossible either.

Struggles have a way of hijacking our ability to look past the current situation. It locks our perspectives into the object of threat. This is basically our mind's way of making sure we pay attention, and there are times when this helps a lot. On the other hand, if we're not careful, this can easily turn into a habit that, when allowed to persist without so much as our awareness or consent, deeply impacts our overall emotional experience and gets in the way of the major life decisions we are about to make.

The antidote? You have to consciously and deliberately decide to stop over-focusing on the object of the threat, step back, and attempt to look at your situation from an outsider's point of view. You can still take a good look at the identified threat, of course—this will let you gather important details about the problem at hand and gain some sort of blueprint that'll help us come up with solutions—just be aware of your natural tendency to ignore information that goes against what you think you know. When you have enough facts from one point of view, you can move on to the next. Try to see things from all sides and see if insight kicks in. Use logic to weigh things. Rely on supporting evidence to draw conclusions. Challenge what you know and cultivate the willingness to be wrong. Be honest, and above all, be patient with yourself. Beating the blues is no easy feat. You may feel quite discouraged some days, and that's okay.

Chapter 9

The Sun Will Come Out Tomorrow

"If life could change for the worst, I thought, then maybe life could change for the better." (Kingslover, 1988, p.232)

Hope doesn't just make us feel good—it urges us on. It keeps our heads above the water and our eyes in front of us. It goes beyond optimism and wishful thinking; it doesn't just imagine a better ending—it expects it. It isn't an emotion born out of inspiration either—it is a state of mind born out of wisdom and courage. Contrary to what most of us might think, hope isn't fuzzy or cheesy at all—it's hardcore, stubborn, and unrelenting. It breeds resilience.

Holocaust survivor Viktor Frankl, for one, went so far as to say that, when people are subjected to extreme conditions, hope determines who dies or lives. Observing his fellow prisoners of war, he saw with his own eyes how the hopeless deteriorated—mentally, physically, and emotionally—under the toughest circumstances and how those who clung to hope, despite the odds, managed to keep on. Simply put, those without hope tend to succumb to adversity, whereas those who cling to it flat-out refuse to cave in. How is this possible? It turns out, as modern research would suggest, that hope keeps us alive in extremely tough times—literally and figuratively. Research by Jerome Groopman, for instance, found that hope doesn't just block pain by releasing certain hormones in the body; it also increases our ability to heal. And that is just remarkable—phenomenal, mind-blowing! If we could only grab hold of hope every time life decides to rock our boat,

Unfortunately, hope doesn't just spring out of the ground like wildflowers. It is a conclusion we arrive at after factoring in every bit of information we have learned about life and ourselves. That said, moving from hopeless to hopeful, couldn't be achieved by mere inspiration. It requires a change of mindset, a shift of focus, and a leap of faith. It requires the courage to be wrong, the readiness to accept disappointment, and the willingness to celebrate. I can tell you, right here, right now: "There is always hope", but unless you decide to muster what it takes to believe that, no amount of coaxing will allow you to have hope.

According to the American Psychological Association, some people are more likely to hope than others (Weir, 2013). This does not mean, however, that struggling to hope means you'll never be able to. You see, hope isn't just a trait; it can be a skill too, and the thing with skills is that you can always do something on your end to buff them up. And hope, once nurtured, is a powerful weapon against adversity. Think of it as a lifeline—you can never go wrong with always keeping one within reach. As Janno White once said, "No storm, not even the one in your life, can last forever. The storm is just passing over."

Chapter 10

Embracing the Shadows

"All the variety, all the charm, all the beauty of life is made up of light and shadow."-Leo Tolstoy

W e cannot do away with shadows and the dark. As much as light appeals to us, too much of it is blinding. The world is made up of hues and blends of endless possibilities; it is never set in a monotone. The same goes for life. The more we understand this, the better we are able to appreciate every experience—the good, the bad, and the strange mixes.

Loneliness can be depressing, depression can be lonely, and nobody wants to get caught in the haywire of emotional turmoil or get stranded in the dull nothingness of anhedonia. These conditions are difficult and seem to defy the very idea of joy. A lot of us have this vague inkling that joy is sun and rainbows, but come to think of it, the most beautiful sun we'll ever see is on the brink of daybreak or on the eve of dusk, where shadows dance with it. Ask any painter about it, and they'd tell you that the best way to make light pop up in their paintings is to enhance the dark tones around them.

So, if you look at your life right now and all you see are dark gray clouds, or if you imagine your inner world's sky and all you see is pitch black, remind yourself that cloud formations shift and a pitch-black sky is still sky—which, when examined closely, harbors within it hundreds or maybe even thousands of tiny glittering diamonds, each one with a story to tell.

Chapter 11

Conclusion

J oy is a precious, profound thing, but the world has made it shallow. It takes a while to recognize its subtlety. It is still elusive, like a unicorn in the midst, but with courage, patience, and calm expectation, it reveals itself.

The world can be a lonely place, even for the merriest soul. Understanding this takes the pressure off our chests and lets us dance with loneliness instead of battling with it. The more you learn to do this, the more your skies will clear, even just a little bit. When that finally happens, hold that tiny patch of blue in your memory. Let it remind you that rain and storms would come and go—sometimes staying longer than we'd like—but underneath all the clouds the sky remains the same, and hope stands.

Author's Note to the Reader

Dear Reader,

If you found this book to be of value, please take five minutes of your time to leave a review on amazon.com. When you no longer have a use for the book please pass it to someone who can benefit from the information. Remember, let kindness be your guide because you never know if the person you meet next is in a bad headspace. You may just turn their day around or save a life.

Thank you,
Paris

References

Ackerman, C. (2017, April 12). *28 Benefits of Gratitude & Most Significant Research Findings.* PositivePsychology.com.

American Psychiatric Association. (2013). *Diagnostic and statistical manual of mental disorders (5th ed.).* American Psychiatric Association.

Arnout, B. A. (2019). The relative contribution of psychological serenity and self-regulated learning strategies in predicting academic engagement among university students. *International Journal of Medical Research & Health Sciences.*

Asana. (2021). *6 Tips to Achieve Flow State at Work.* Asana.

Basile, B., Mancini, F., Macaluso, E., Caltagirone, C., Frackowiak, R. S. J., & Bozzali, M. (2010). Deontological and altruistic guilt: evidence for distinct neurobiological substrates. *Human Brain Mapping, 32*(2), 229–239.

Bhandari, S. (2020). *What Is Anhedonia?* WebMD.

Brain Basics: Know Your Brain. (n.d.). National Institute of Neurological Disorders and Stroke. Retrieved April 22, 2023, from Carol Shaw Austad. (2009). *Counseling and psychotherapy today: theory, practice, and research.* McGraw-Hill Higher Education.

CCI - *Anxiety, Depression, Bipolar & Eating Disorders - Perth.* (2019). Wa.gov.au.

Cherry, K. (2021). *Why Toxic Positivity Can Be So Harmful.* Verywell Mind.

Chilton, D. (2019). *8 Signs You Have an Unhealthy Work-life Balance.* Denise Chilton Coaching.

Chowdhury, M. R. (2019). *The Neuroscience of Gratitude and How it Affects Anxiety and Grief.* PositivePsychology.com.

Contributors, W. E. (2021). *What is Gestalt Therapy?* WebMD.

Davidson, K. (2021). *Laughing Yoga: What is It and Does It Work?* Healthline.

DD, K. S. L. (2023). *How to Deal with Guilt: 14 Tips for Coping.* Talkspace.

De Saint-Exupéry, A. (1943). *The little prince.* Ancient Wisdom Publications.

Deng, P. (2020). *Why It's Okay to Ask for Help: Change Your Mind, Change Your Life.*

Denning, T. (2020). *No One Can Take Away from You What You've Put in Your Own Mind.* Ascent Publication.

Der-Avakian, A. & Markou, A. (2012). The neurobiology of anhedonia and other reward-related deficits. *Trends In Neurosciences,* 35(1), 68–77.

Drake, K. (2021, November 15). *Toxic People and How to Deal with Them.* Psych Central.

DriveThru Team. (2020). *15 Celebrities Speak Out with These Mental Health Quotes.* DiveThru.

Dsquared. (2020). *A Guide to the Ins and Outs of DBT Therapy.* Delray Center for Healing.

Eerola, T. & Peltola, H.R. (2016). Memorable experiences with sad music—reasons, reactions and mechanisms of three types of experiences. *PLOS ONE,* 11(6), e0157444.

Faraaz Kazi Quotes. (n.d.). Quotefancy.com. Retrieved April 22, 2023, from Frankl, V. E. (2006). *Man's search for meaning.* Beacon Press.

Fredrickson, B. (2001). The role of positive emotions in positive psychology. *The American Psychologist,* 56(3), 218–226. https://www.ncbi.nlm.nih.gov/pmc/articles/PMC3122271/

George Bernard Shaw Quotes. (n.d.). BrainyQuote. Retrieved April 22, 2023, from https://www.brainyquote.com/quotes/george_bernard_shaw_120971

Gillette, H. (2022). What is Guilt? Signs, Causes, and How to Cope. Psych Central. https://psychcentral.com/health/what-is-guilt

Glasser, W. (2014). Choice theory: a new psychology of personal freedom. HarperCollins e-Books.

Gluck, S. (2020). *Depression Quotes & Sayings That Capture Life with Depression.* HealthyPlace.

https://www.healthyplace.com/insight/quotes/depression-qu
otes-and-sayings-about-depression.

Green, J. (2012). *The fault in our stars.* Dutton Books.

Greene, C. (n.d.). *Laugh with Celeste.* Celeste Greene Laughs:
Atlanta Laughter Yoga Teacher. Retrieved April 22, 2023, from
Guo, L. (2023). *Anhedonia What is It, Causes, Diagnosis, and
More.*

Health (UK), N. C. C. for M. (2010). *The Classification of
Depression and Depression Rating Scales/Questionnaires.* British
Psychological Society.

Heshmat, S. (n.d.). *The 5 Key Elements of Aesthetic Experience.*
Psychology Today United Kingdom. Retrieved April 22,
2023, from Heshmat, S. (2017). *Seeing the Bigger Picture Can
Promote Self-Control.* Psychology Today.

Hoffman, L. (2018). *Existential Guilt.* Encyclopedia of
Psychology and Religion, 1–3.

How to Achieve Flow State. (n.d.). Routine. Retrieved April
22, 2023, from *How to Laugh in the Face of Stress.* (2019).
Verywell Mind.
https://www.verywellmind.com/maintain-a-sense-of-humor
-3144888.

Huxler, M. (2020). *Serenity Meditation: On the Pathway to Awakening.* Insight Timer Blog.

Internal Family Systems Therapy. (2013). Psychology Today.

Irvine, W. B. (2009). *A guide to the good life: the ancient art of stoic joy.* Oxford University Press.

Iyanla Vanzant Quote. (n.d.) Retrieved April 22, 2023, from Jandrić, P. (2022). Alone-time and loneliness in the academia. *Postdigital Science and Education.*

Kingsolver, B. (2013). *The bean trees:* a novel. Harper Perennial.

Komulainen, E., Meskanen, K., Lipsanen, J., Lahti, J. M., Jylhä, P., Melartin, T., Wichers, M., Isometsä, E. & Ekelund, J. (2014). The Effect of Personality on Daily Life Emotional Processes. *PLoS ONE, 9*(10), e110907.

L'Engle, M. (2008). *A ring of endless light.* Farrar, Straus and Giroux (BYR).

Lamia, M. (2011). *Loneliness Has a Purpose.* Psychology Today.

Leder, H. & Nadal, M. (2014). Ten years of a model of aesthetic appreciation and aesthetic judgments: The aesthetic episode - developments and challenges in empirical aesthetics. *British Journal of Psychology,* 105(4), 443–464.

Leonard, J. (2020). *Mood Swings: What Are They? Causes In Males and Females, and More.* Www.medicalnewstoday.com.

Light, N. (n.d.). *Is It Normal to Feel Like This?* Naomi Light. Retrieved April 22, 2023, from LMSW Wilding, M. (2021). *Trust yourself, stop overthinking and channel your emotions for success at work.* Chronicle Books LLC.

Logan, A. (2022). *Can Expressing Gratitude Improve Health?* Mayo Clinic Health System.

Lonczak, H. (2020). *Humor in Psychology: Coping and Laughing Your Woes Away.* PositivePsychology.com.

Lucille, A.W. (n.d.). *Online IFS Therapy Sessions, Jungian Analysis & Art Therapy.* Seek Deeply | Jungian Therapy and IFS Coaching Online. Retrieved April 22, 2023, from Lumley, M. A., Schubiner, H., Lockhart, N. A., Kidwell, K. M., Harte, S. E., Clauw, D. J. & Williams, D. A. (2017). Emotional awareness and expression therapy, cognitive behavioral therapy, and education for fibromyalgia. *PAIN,* 158(12), 2354–2363.

Mayo Clinic. (n.d.). *How To Stop Negative Self-talk.* Mayo Clinic. Retrieved April 22, 2023, from McCallum, W. C. (2019). *Attention Psychology.* Encyclopædia Britannica.

Morin, A. (2019). *How Cognitive Reframing is Used in Mental Health.* Verywell Mind.

Nakamura, J. & Csikszentmihalyi, M. (2002). *APA PsycNet.* Psycnet.apa.org.

Overview Depression in Adults: Treatment and Management. (2022). National Institute for Health and Care Excellence UK.

Schondelmayer, L. (2021). *New Study Finds That the Older We Get, The More Grateful We Are.* College of Social Science, Michigan State University. https://socialscience.msu.edu/news-events/news/2022-01-05.html

Non-Drug Pain Management. (n.d.). Medlineplus.gov. Retrieved April 22, 2023, from Novotney, A. (2019). *The Risks Of Social Isolation.* American Psychological Association.

Nutt, D., Wilson, S., & Paterson, L. (2008). Sleep disorders as core symptoms of depression. *Dialogues in Clinical Neuroscience, 10*(3), 329–336.

Oli, P. (2016). *In Memory Of Umberto Eco.* The Edge. https://www.theedgesusu.co.uk/features/2016/02/23/to-survi ve-you-must-tell-stories-in-memory-of-umberto-eco/Pattak os, A. (2018). *Search for Meaning as the Basic Human Motivation.* Psychology Today. https://www.psychologytoday.com/intl/blog/the-meaningful -life/201807/search-meaning-the-basic-human-motivation.

Posner, M. (2021). *Leonard Cohen, untold stories: from this broken hill, volume 2.* Simon and Schuster.

Purse, M. (2023). *Bipolar Depression Often Blunts Your Physical and Mental Skills.* Verywell Mind. https://www.verywellmind.com/psychomotor-retardation-38 0166 .

R. Marasigan, P. (2019). Using brief cognitive restructuring and cognitive defusion techniques to cope with negative thoughts. *Social Values & Society* (SVS), 1(4), 11–14. https://econpapers.repec.org/article/zibzbnsvs/v_3a1_3ay_3a2 019_3ai_3a3_3ap_3a11-14.htm

Randy Pausch Quote. (n.d.) Retrieved April 22, 2023, from Robinson, L., Smith, M. & Segal, J. (2018). *Laughter is the Best Medicine.* Help Guide.

Rodenhizer, S. (2018). *Joseph Newton Quotes.* Quotation Celebration.

Rothenberg, M. (2002). *Children with emerald eyes: histories of extraordinary boys & girls.* North Atlantic Books; Lyons, Colo.

Rubin, K. & Barstead, M. (2018). *Social Withdrawal and Solitude.* ResearchGate.

Russell, E. & Fosha, D. (2008). Transformational affects and core state in AEDP: the emergence and consolidation of joy, hope, gratitude, and confidence in (the solid goodness of) the self. *Journal of Psychotherapy Integration,* 18(2), 167–190.

Sanfilippo, M. (2023). *How to Improve Your Work-Life Balance.* Business News Daily.

Schwartz, R. C. (2021). *No bad parts: healing trauma and restoring wholeness with the internal family systems model.* Sounds True.

Scott, R. (Director). (1997). *G.I. Jane [Movie].* Hollywood Pictures.

Smith, E.M. (n.d.). *Positivity for Depression: Is That Even Possible?* HealthyPlace. Retrieved April 22, 2023, from Stewart,

J. (n.d.). *How to Distinguish Healthy Positivity From Toxic Positivity.*

School Coaching Mastery. Retrieved April 22, 2023, from SWNS. (2020). *Is Acting Spontaneously the Key to Happiness?* https://nypost.com/2020/06/11/is-acting-spontaneously-the-key-to-happiness/

Theobald, M. (2013). *Depression, Memory Loss, and Concentration.* Everyday Health.

Tolstoy, L. (2016). *Anna karenina.* Xist Publishing.

Timalsina, S. (2013). Gauḍapāda on Imagination. *Journal of Indian Philosophy, 41*(6), 591–602.

Using Humor and Play to Overcome Challenges and Enhance Your Life. (n.d.). Well Life Family Medicine. Retrieved April 22, 2023, from Wang, A., McCarron, R., Azzam, D., Stehli, A., Xiong, G. & DeMartini, J. (2021). *Utilizing Big Data from Google Trends to Map Out Population Depression in the United States: Exploratory Infodemiology Study (Preprint).* JMIR Mental Health.

Wang, J., Wu, X., Lai, W., Long, E., Zhang, X., Li, W., Zhu, Y., Chen, C., Zhong, X., Liu, Z., Wang, D. & Lin, H. (2017). Prevalence of depression and depressive symptoms among outpatients: a systematic review and meta-analysis. *BMJ Open, 7*(8), e017173.

Webster Merriam. (1964). *Webster's new practical school dictionary; a new dictionary for boys and girls, a Merriam Webster.* American Book, Co.

Weir, K. (2013). *Mission Impossible.* Https://Www.apa.org.

When One Door Closes, Does Another One Really Open? (n.d.). Ironmountaindailynews.com. Retrieved April 22, 2023, from Wilson, L. (2018). *6 Different Types of Depression and How They Are Treated.* SACAP.

Worldwide, A. S. (n.d.). *How Do I Safely Finish a Meditation?* Ananda. Retrieved April 22, 2023, from Wurtzel, E. (1995). *Prozac nation.* New York: Riverhead Books.

Yamagishi, A. (2014, January). *Four Types of Guilt and Guilt in the Japanese.* ResearchGate.

About Author

Paris Bailey is an author who has always been passionate about good books. With a love of literature and a curious mind, she is making a name for herself as an indie author. Paris thrives on the challenge of stretching herself, both personally and professionally. She enjoys exploring new ideas and perspectives, always eager to expand her knowledge and understanding of the world.

Paris can be found chasing her grandkids around the house when she's not writing or researching. She cherishes her time with her family and friends.

In her downtime, Paris enjoys traveling with her husband. She finds inspiration in exploring new places and experiencing new cultures. Paris especially likes lounging on a beach collecting her thoughts but is always up for an adventure.

Printed in Great Britain
by Amazon

38406647R00089